e Open
iversity

irst level
disciplinary
course

Using **Mathematics**

BLOCK C
CONTINUOUS MODELS

Integration and modelling

Prepared by the course team

APTER

About this course

This course, MST121 *Using Mathematics*, and the courses MU120 *Open Mathematics* and MS221 *Exploring Mathematics* provide a flexible means of entry to university-level mathematics. Further details may be obtained from the Course Reservations and Sales Centre (see address below).

MST121 uses the software program Mathcad (MathSoft, Inc.) and other software to investigate mathematical and statistical concepts and as a tool in problem solving. This software is provided as part of the course, and its use is covered in the associated Computer Book.

The Open University, Walton Hall, Milton Keynes, MK7 6AA.

First published 1997. Reprinted 1997

Edited, designed and typeset by the Open University using the Open University TEX System.

Printed in the United Kingdom by Caligraving Limited, Thetford, Norfolk.

ISBN 0 7492 7865 X

This text forms part of an Open University First Level Course. If you would like a copy of *Studying with The Open University*, please write to the Course Reservations and Sales Centre, PO Box 724, The Open University, Walton Hall, Milton Keynes, MK7 6ZS. If you have not already enrolled on the Course and would like to buy this or other Open University material, please write to Open University Educational Enterprises Ltd, 12 Cofferidge Close, Stony Stratford, Milton Keynes, MK11 1BY, United Kingdom.

1.2

Contents

Study guide   4

Introduction   5

1   The basics of integration   7
   1.1   Undoing differentiation   7
   1.2   Integration by guesswork   12

2   Integration with Mathcad   23
   2.1   Integrating simpler functions   23
   2.2   Integrating more complicated functions   23

3   Differential equations and applications   25
   3.1   General and particular solutions   25
   3.2   Motion with constant acceleration   29
   3.3   Population growth and radioactive decay   35

4   Definite integrals, areas and summations   44
   4.1   Areas under graphs and the definite integral   44
   4.2   The definite integral as a limit of summations   52
   4.3   Definite integrals in Mathcad   57

5   Further applications of definite integrals   59
   5.1   Population in a town   59
   5.2   Flow in a circular pipe   63

Summary of Chapter C2   69
   Learning outcomes   69

Solutions to Activities   72

Solutions to Exercises   78

Study guide

This chapter is longer than average, and you should schedule six study sessions for your work on it. In the first of these you will need access to an audio-cassette player, while the second and fifth require use of the computer (unless you schedule your studies otherwise, as suggested below).

The study pattern which we recommend is as follows.

Study session 1: Section 1. You will need access to your audio-cassette player for the second and more substantial part of this session. The session will probably require more study time than most of the later ones.

Study session 2: Section 2. You will need access to your computer for all of this session, together with Computer Book C. However, there are no Mathcad files associated with this session.

Study session 3: Subsections 3.1 and 3.2.

Study session 4: Subsections 3.3 and 4.1. This session will probably require more study time than most of the others.

Study session 5: Subsections 4.2 and 4.3. There are no activities in Subsection 4.2, since the computer is required for practical implementation of what is discussed here. You will need access to your computer for Subsection 4.3, together with the Mathcad disk for Block C and Computer Book C.

Study session 6: Section 5.

An alternative pattern is possible in respect of Section 2 and Subsection 4.3, which involve the use of the computer. Section 2 can be studied at any stage after Subsection 1.2, while Subsection 4.3 can be studied at any time after Subsection 4.2 provided that Section 2 has also been covered. This means that the study of the main text of the chapter is not affected by whether you have studied those parts which require the computer in the recommended sequence. You might therefore choose to take all of the computer-related work in a long session or two shorter ones towards the end of your study of the chapter.

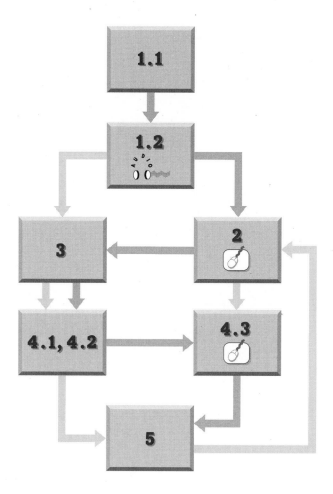

Introduction

In this chapter we continue to use calculus to model situations which involve continuous change. As explained in the block Introduction, calculus has two main branches, called *differentiation* and *integration*. Chapter C1 was concerned with the first of these, and showed how the process of differentiation can be used to answer questions such as the following: How fast is something changing? Is it increasing or decreasing? Does it ever stop changing, permanently or temporarily?

In the block Introduction, these questions were accompanied by two others: How does the change accumulate? How can the change be described by an equation? Study of the process of integration will enable us to answer the first of these questions, and to 'solve' equations of the type referred to in the second question, which are known as *differential equations*.

An example of 'accumulating change' is provided by the relationship between the velocity of a car and its position at any time. You saw in Chapter C1 that the instantaneous velocity of an object, such as a car, can be calculated by differentiating its position function with respect to time. We are now interested in reversing this direction of development, and considering how much can be deduced about the car's position from knowledge of its velocity function. Here the velocity is the rate of change of position, and the total change of position over some time interval is, roughly speaking, the accumulation of all the instantaneous changes which take place during the interval. It is integration which makes precise what is meant by an 'accumulation of instantaneous changes', and hence enables progress to be made in this situation.

As suggested by this example, integration is a process which 'undoes' or reverses the effect of differentiation, and it is from this point of view that we start to study integration. The 'accumulation' aspect can be seen initially as a separate way of looking at integration, though the link between these two approaches is of fundamental importance.

In Section 1 the idea of integration as an 'undoing' of differentiation is first introduced informally. The outcome of integrating a function is called its *integral* and, in an audio-tape session, you will see how the integral can be determined for a range of standard functions. More complicated functions may be integrated with the aid of Mathcad, and you are invited to investigate this in Section 2.

Section 3 shows how differential equations, that is, equations which involve derivatives, arise in mathematical models, and how integration may be used to solve them.

A new light is cast on integration in Section 4, where a distinction is drawn between the *indefinite* integral considered so far and the so-called *definite* integral. Correspondingly, the emphasis shifts from integration as the 'undoing' of differentiation to integration as an 'accumulation of changes', as discussed briefly above. You will see that one application of the definite integral is to find areas which are bounded above by the graph of the function being integrated. This in turn leads on to the idea of an integral as an 'infinite sum'. Further applications of definite integrals are given in Section 5.

The learning skills themes that were introduced in Chapter C1 continue through this chapter, with particular emphasis on how communicating meaning can help in understanding. When we ask you to summarise what you have learned it may be helpful to imagine that you are explaining the ideas to another MST121 student. In mathematics, an important aspect of communication is the use of accepted notation, and attention is paid to practising reading as an aid to using the notation of integration appropriately.

Communicating with yourself—being aware of what you are doing and why you are doing it as you work on mathematics—can also be helpful in increasing your understanding. In this chapter it may be particularly useful to work on being aware of the stages of the modelling process. As you read the chapter and work through the examples and activities, pause to reflect on where you are in the modelling cycle, perhaps adding annotations in the margins where this has not already been done.

1 The basics of integration

To study Subsection 1.2, you will need Audio Tape 3 and access to your audio player.

The idea of integration as an 'undoing' of differentiation is introduced informally in Subsection 1.1, with reference to an example which you saw in Chapter C1, namely, the motion of an object falling freely under the effect of gravity. The outcome of integrating a function is called its *integral*. You will see in Subsection 1.2 how the integral may be found for a range of standard functions. The techniques of integration are best assimilated through plenty of practice, so you will find that there is a good supply of activities to be worked through here.

Chapter C1 Subsection 4.3

1.1 Undoing differentiation

In Chapter C1 Subsection 4.3, you were asked to consider the motion of a falling object. A standard model was introduced for an object which falls vertically, starting from rest, and is acted upon only by the force of gravity. You saw that, in this model, the downward velocity v m s^{-1} of the object at time t seconds after the start of the motion is given by

$$v = 9.8t.$$

From this expression, it is possible to calculate the acceleration of the object, since the acceleration is the derivative of the velocity. Thus the acceleration a m s^{-2} of the object is

$$a = \frac{dv}{dt} = \frac{d}{dt}(9.8t) = 9.8.$$

The constant acceleration 9.8 m s^{-2} is characteristic of any object which falls under gravity alone, that is, with the effects of any other forces such as air resistance being ignored.

Suppose now that we wish instead to deduce the velocity of a freely falling object from its acceleration. We start this time from the knowledge that the acceleration is $a = 9.8$ m s^{-2}, and that a and the velocity v m s^{-1} are related by the equation

$$\frac{dv}{dt} = a.$$

In other words, we seek an expression for v for which

$$\frac{dv}{dt} = 9.8.$$

A solution in this case is not hard to find, because of the way in which the example was set up; the function $v = 9.8t$ is such a solution.

What we have done here is to 'undo' or 'reverse' the process of differentiation which takes us from the velocity v to the acceleration a. This 'undoing' of differentiation can be regarded as a process in its own right, and it is called **integration**. The outcome of integrating is called an **integral**, so that $v = 9.8t$ is an integral of $dv/dt = 9.8$.

This may seem very straightforward so far, but matters can be harder to resolve when an integral is not effectively given in advance as in this case. For example, we might be told that an object attached to the end of a spring oscillates with the acceleration $a = dv/dt = \cos t$. What velocity can the object have? On the basis of what you have seen about differentiation, you may be able to deduce that a possible velocity function in this case is $v = \sin t$, because $\cos t$ is the derivative of $\sin t$, but this requires more thought than the first example.

Reverting to the case of an object falling freely under gravity, for which an integral $v = 9.8t$ was found above, the following question can be asked:

Is $v = 9.8t$ the *only* possible integral of $dv/dt = 9.8$?

An alternative way of phrasing this question is as follows:

Is $v = 9.8t$ the *only* function whose derivative is $dv/dt = 9.8$?

The activity below invites you to investigate this question.

Activity 1.1   *What changes? What stays the same?*

Differentiate each of the following velocity functions. What do you notice?

(a) $v = 9.8t$ (b) $v = 9.8t + 2$ (c) $v = \sqrt{5} + 9.8t$

(d) $v = 9.8t - \pi$

Comment

Solutions are given on page 72.

The outcome of Activity 1.1 suggests that there are many functions whose derivative is $dv/dt = 9.8$, and indeed that any function of the form $v = 9.8t + c$, where c is a constant, will fit the bill. It turns out that this expression for v gives *all* of the functions whose derivative is 9.8. We say that $v = 9.8t + c$ is the *indefinite integral* of $dv/dt = 9.8$.

This demonstrates one respect in which integration is somewhat more than simply 'undoing differentiation'. On differentiating a given function, we obtain a unique derivative, but on integrating a given function we are faced with an infinite set of possible functions.

These facts have an interpretation in the context of falling objects. If the velocity function of such an object is known, then its acceleration is uniquely determined. On the other hand, we have said that any object in free fall has the same acceleration $dv/dt = 9.8$, for which the indefinite integral is $v = 9.8t + c$, where c is a constant. Thus any object in free fall must have a velocity function of the form $v = 9.8t + c$, but this includes many possibilities besides the originally specified velocity function $v = 9.8t$ (for which $c = 0$).

One way to distinguish between all of these possible velocity functions is to note that the constant c is in each case the value of v at the starting time, $t = 0$. It follows that, by choosing an appropriate value for c, we can obtain the particular velocity function for an object in free fall which has the initial velocity $v = c$. Since any real number gives a possible initial velocity (in $m\,s^{-1}$), the equation $v = 9.8t + c$ describes the velocities of all possible vertical motions in free fall.

Example 1.1   Finding the particular velocity

Suppose that a film scene requires a person to perform a vertical bungee jump. The scene is expected to last for about two seconds after the initial jump, with the person falling freely during this time, that is, the elastic rope does not become taut during the first two seconds of the jump. The person who performs the jump pushes themselves off downwards with an initial velocity of 3 m s^{-1}. Estimate the velocity of the person 2 seconds after the jump starts.

Solution

Since the jumper is in free fall, the acceleration (measured in the downward direction) is given by $dv/dt = 9.8$ (in m s^{-2}). The velocity function must therefore be of the form

$$v = 9.8t + c,$$

for some value of the constant c. Taking $t = 0$ at the start of the jump, we have $c = 3$ (the initial velocity, in m s^{-1}). Hence the velocity function of the jumper is

$$v = 9.8t + 3,$$

and after 2 seconds, their velocity is

$$9.8 \times 2 + 3 = 22.6 \, \text{m s}^{-1}.$$

We now seek to generalise the mathematical development which led above to the obtaining of possible velocity functions from a given acceleration. Suppose that f is any function, and that F is a function whose derivative is equal to f, that is,

$$F' = f \quad \text{or} \quad \frac{d}{dt}F(t) = f(t). \tag{1.1}$$

Then F is called **an integral** of f. As with the case of velocities above, there is more than one possible choice for the function $F(t)$ which satisfies equation (1.1). If $F(t)$ is one such function, and c is any constant, then $F(t) + c$ also has derivative $f(t)$. This follows from the Sum Rule for derivatives, since we have

Chapter C1 Subsection 3.2

$$\frac{d}{dt}(F(t) + c) = \frac{d}{dt}(F(t)) + \frac{d}{dt}(c) = f(t) + 0 = f(t).$$

In fact, the expression $F(t) + c$, where c is any constant, represents all of the functions whose derivative is $f(t)$. We call $F(t) + c$ **the indefinite integral** of $f(t)$. Since the constant c can take any value, it is described as an *arbitrary* constant, or as the *constant of integration*.

Thus, if $F(t)$ is any one function whose derivative is $f(t)$, then $F(t)$ is called *an* integral of $f(t)$, while the expression $F(t) + c$, denoting all functions whose derivative is $f(t)$, is called *the indefinite* integral of $f(t)$. This indefinite integral is denoted by

The words 'antiderivative' and 'primitive' are sometimes used for what we refer to here as an integral.

$$\int f \quad \text{or} \quad \int f(t) \, dt,$$

so we may write

$$\int f(t) \, dt = F(t) + c,$$

where c is an arbitrary constant.

For our previous example, with the acceleration $f(t) = 9.8$ and an integral (possible velocity) $F(t) = 9.8t$, the indefinite integral (most general possible velocity function) is

$$\int 9.8 \, dt = 9.8t + c,$$

where c is an arbitrary constant.

When finding the indefinite integral of a function $f(t)$, it is natural to make the simplest possible choice for the function $F(t)$ (an integral of $f(t)$), and then to add the '$+c$' to this. This is demonstrated in the example below.

Example 1.2   Finding an indefinite integral

Find the indefinite integral of the function

$$f(t) = 2t.$$

Solution

The key to solving this problem is to identify a function $F(t)$ whose derivative is equal to the given function $f(t) = 2t$. As you may recall from Chapter C1, we have

$$\frac{d}{dt}(t^2) = 2t,$$

and so $F(t) = t^2$ is one possibility. There are others ($t^2 + 1$, for example), but t^2 is the simplest.

Thus the indefinite integral of $f(t) = 2t$ is given by

$$\int 2t \, dt = t^2 + c,$$

where c is an arbitrary constant.

This answer may be checked by differentiating it. The outcome should be (and is) the function $2t$ whose indefinite integral we set out to find. Any other indefinite integral can be checked in a similar manner.

The effect of the indefinite integral operation

$$\int \ldots \, dt$$

is to undo the effect of the differentiation operation represented by d/dt though, as you have seen, it also entails the addition of an arbitrary constant. The symbol $\int$ is called the *integral sign*. It is an old-fashioned elongated 'S', standing for the word 'sum'. The connection between integrals and sums will become apparent later in the chapter. The function which takes the place of the ... above is called the *integrand*, that is, the function to be *integrated*. The pair of symbols dt on the end of the integral notation indicate that the integration in this case is to be performed with respect to the variable t.

Integration may of course be performed with respect to other variables. For example,

$$\int \ldots \, dx$$

represents an integration with respect to the variable x, which 'undoes' the effect of d/dx. Thus, from the result of the integration in Example 1.2, we have

$$\int 2x \, dx = x^2 + c,$$

where c is an arbitrary constant.

We have defined 'the indefinite integral' of a function above. Later in the chapter, you will see that there is a different type of entity which is named the *definite* integral. However, until it becomes necessary to make the distinction between these two types of integral, we shall often omit the adjective 'indefinite' and refer simply to 'the integral'.

When the notations for derivatives were introduced in Chapter C1, you were encouraged to try and pronounce them out loud, since this is psychologically important for assimilation and necessary in order to talk about the topic with others. The same applies where the integral notation is concerned. The collection of symbols

Chapter C1 Subsection 2.3

$$\int f(x) \, dx$$

is pronounced as 'the integral of f of x with respect to x' or simply as 'the integral of f of x dee-x'.

Activity 1.2   *Saying it out loud*

It is often quite tricky to 'read' mathematics from a textbook simply because of the symbols and notation. Being able to read symbols aloud can be very helpful. As in Chapter C1, we suggest that you spend some time saying to yourself

(a) 'the integral of y dee-y' for $\int y \, dy$;

(b) 'the integral of z squared dee-z' for $\int z^2 \, dz$;

(c) 'the integral of g of t dee-t' for $\int g(t) \, dt$.

Comment

As with derivatives, you should find it much easier to remember and use the notation if you can also say it. If you feel the need of further practice, then there are plenty of examples in the rest of the chapter. You will also be able to practise from here on as you continue with the text.

Activity 1.3   *Understanding new ideas*

You have just been introduced to the new idea of integration. Summarise in your own words, on Learning File Sheet 1, what the connection is between differentiation and integration. It may be helpful to imagine that you are writing your summary for a fellow MST121 student. Spend some time studying the symbols which make up the integral notation, and make sure that you understand it.

Suppose that

$$h(x) = \int f(x) \, dx.$$

What is $h'(x)$?

Comment

We know that

$$\int f(x)\,dx = F(x) + c,$$

where c is an arbitrary constant and $F(x)$ is any function such that $F'(x) = f(x)$. Hence we have

$$h'(x) = \frac{d}{dx}(F(x) + c) = F'(x) = f(x).$$

This subsection has introduced the idea of integration as an 'undoing' of differentiation. The next embarks on the task of actually finding the integrals for a variety of functions.

1.2 Integration by guesswork

In Example 1.2, we integrated the function $2t$ by recalling from Chapter C1 that one function with derivative $2t$ is t^2. In other cases, the power of recall may not suffice to produce an integral, or the function to be integrated may not be in a form which has been seen previously as the derivative of another function.

In such a situation, one important approach is to make a guess at an answer! The form of the original function may suggest roughly what type of guess to make. Any guess can be checked by differentiating it, and seeing whether the derivative is indeed the function for which an integral is sought. If it is, then well and good: an integral has been identified. Otherwise, a further guess may be attempted, possibly with an improved chance of success as a result of comparing the derivative of the first guess with the original function.

This 'guess and check' approach is profitable precisely because integration has the effect of 'undoing' differentiation, and because you have already built up a body of knowledge concerning derivatives which can be called upon in the checking phase.

In this subsection you will see how the guesswork method of integration can provide us with integrals for certain standard functions, leading to the construction of a basic table of integrals. You will also see that some of the rules for differentiation can be translated into rules for integration, which extend your ability to integrate beyond the results in the table.

Now listen to Audio Tape 3, Band 2, 'Integration by guesswork'.

FRAME 1

Reversing differentiation

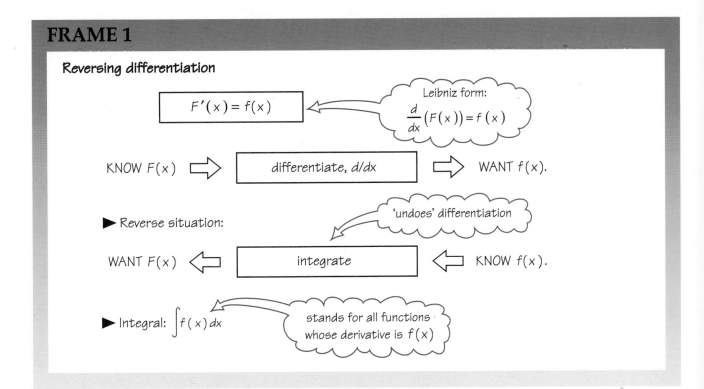

FRAME 2

Each function has many 'integrals'

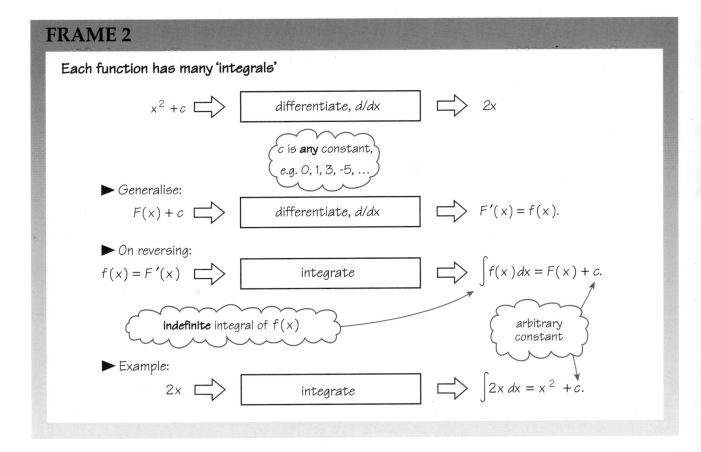

FRAME 3

A table of derivatives

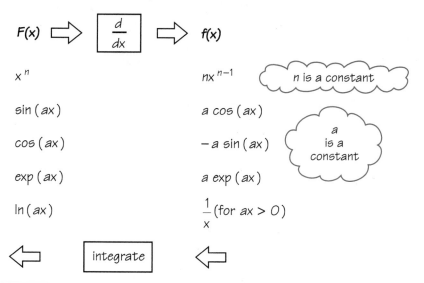

$$F(x) \implies \boxed{\frac{d}{dx}} \implies f(x)$$

$F(x)$	$f(x)$	
x^n	nx^{n-1}	*n is a constant*
$\sin(ax)$	$a\cos(ax)$	
$\cos(ax)$	$-a\sin(ax)$	*a is a constant*
$\exp(ax)$	$a\exp(ax)$	
$\ln(ax)$	$\dfrac{1}{x}$ (for $ax > 0$)	

$$\Longleftarrow \boxed{\text{integrate}} \Longleftarrow$$

FRAME 4

Using the table to integrate

▶ What is $\displaystyle\int \cos(x)\,dx$?

$$\frac{d}{dx}(\sin(x)) = \cos(x),$$

$f(x) = \cos x$; $a = 1$ in Row 2 of table

$$\text{so } \int \cos(x)\,dx = \sin(x) + c.$$

arbitrary constant

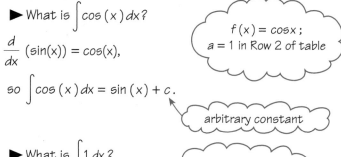

▶ What is $\displaystyle\int 1\,dx$?

$$\frac{d}{dx}(x) = 1,$$

$f(x) = 1$; $n = 1$ in Row 1 of table NB: $x^0 = 1$ and $x^1 = x$

$$\text{so } \int 1\,dx = x + c.$$

arbitrary constant

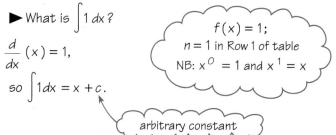

FRAME 5

Three integrals for you to do

▶ What is $\int 3x^2\,dx$?

$$\frac{d}{dx}\left(\boxed{}\right) = 3x^2\text{ , so }\int 3x^2\,dx = \boxed{}.$$

▶ What is $\int nx^{n-1}\,dx$?

$$\frac{d}{dx}\left(\boxed{}\right) = nx^{n-1}\text{ , so }\int nx^{n-1}\,dx = \boxed{}.$$

> Special case $n = 0$: $\int 0\,dx = c.$

▶ What is $\int \frac{1}{x}\,dx$ (for $x > 0$)?

$$\frac{d}{dx}\left(\boxed{}\right) = \frac{1}{x}\quad (a > 0, x > 0),$$

so $\int \frac{1}{x}\,dx = \boxed{}.$

> also expressible as
> $\ln(x) + c$, where $c = \ln(a)$.

FRAME 6

Integrals not in the table

▶ What is $\int x^4\,dx$?

> $5x^4$ is in table; nx^{n-1} with $n = 5$.

$$\frac{d}{dx}\left(x^5\right) = 5x^4.$$

> Use Constant Multiple Rule:
> $$\frac{d}{dx}(bF(x)) = b\frac{d}{dx}(F(x)).$$

Guess: **Check:**

$\dfrac{x^5}{5}$ $\dfrac{d}{dx}\left(\dfrac{x^5}{5}\right) = \dfrac{1}{5}\dfrac{d}{dx}\left(x^5\right) = \dfrac{1}{5}\left(5x^4\right) = x^4.$

So $\int x^4\,dx = \dfrac{x^5}{5} + c.$

▶ What is $\int \sin(x)\,dx$?

$$\frac{d}{dx}(\cos(x)) = -\sin(x).$$ > from table

Guess: **Check:**

$-\cos(x)$ $\dfrac{d}{dx}(-\cos(x)) = -1 \times (-\sin(x)) = \sin(x).$

So $\int \sin(x)\,dx = -\cos(x) + c.$

FRAME 7

The integral of x^n

▶ What is $\int x^n \, dx$?

First guess:

x^{n+1}

Check:

$\dfrac{d}{dx}\left(x^{n+1}\right) = (n+1)x^n$.

> Replace n by $n+1$ in Row 1 of table

Second guess:

Check:

So $\int x^n \, dx =$

> Does this hold for all n?

FRAME 8

The integral of an exponential function

▶ What is $\int \exp(3x) \, dx$?

$\exp(3x) = e^{3x}$

$\dfrac{d}{dx}(\exp(3x)) = 3\exp(3x).$

> from table

Guess:

Check:

So $\int \exp(3x) \, dx =$

FRAME 9

Three for you to try

▶ What is $\int \exp(ax)\,dx$?

$\dfrac{d}{dx}\left(\boxed{}\right)=\boxed{}$ ⟨ from table ⟩

Guess: $\boxed{}$ Check: $\boxed{}$

So $\int \exp(ax)\,dx =\boxed{}$ ⟨ $a \neq 0$ ⟩

▶ What is $\int \sin(ax)\,dx$?

$\dfrac{d}{dx}\left(\boxed{}\right)=\boxed{}$ ⟨ from table ⟩

Guess: $\boxed{}$ Check: $\boxed{}$

So $\int \sin(ax)\,dx =\boxed{}$.   ⟨ $a \neq 0$ ⟩

▶ What is $\int \cos(ax)\,dx$?

$\dfrac{d}{dx}\left(\boxed{}\right)=\boxed{}$ ⟨ from table ⟩

Guess: $\boxed{}$ Check: $\boxed{}$

So $\int \cos(ax)\,dx =\boxed{}$.   ⟨ $a \neq 0$ ⟩

FRAME 10

A table of integrals

$$f(x) \Rightarrow \boxed{\text{integrate}} \Rightarrow \int f(x)\,dx$$

⟨ a and n are constants ⟩

$f(x)$	$\int f(x)\,dx$
a	$ax + c$
$x^n\ (n \neq -1)$	$\dfrac{1}{n+1}x^{n+1} + c$
$\dfrac{1}{x}\ (x > 0)$	$\ln(x) + c$
$\exp(ax)$	$\dfrac{1}{a}\exp(ax) + c$
$\cos(ax)$	$\dfrac{1}{a}\sin(ax) + c$
$\sin(ax)$	$-\dfrac{1}{a}\cos(ax) + c$

⟨ $a \neq 0$ ⟩

⟨ In each case, c is an arbitrary constant ⟩

FRAME 11

Combining results

▶ What is $\int (\exp(3x) + \sin(6x))\, dx$?

From table:

(a) $\exp(3x)$ has an
   integral
   $\frac{1}{3}\exp(3x)$;   [also in Frame 8]

(b) $\sin(6x)$ has an
   integral
   $-\frac{1}{6}\cos(6x)$.   [$a = 6$ in table]

Guess: $\frac{1}{3}\exp(3x) - \frac{1}{6}\cos(6x)$.

Check: $\frac{d}{dx}\left(\frac{1}{3}\exp(3x) - \frac{1}{6}\cos(6x)\right)$

[Sum Rule:
$\frac{d}{dx}(F(x) + G(x))$
$= \frac{d}{dx}(F(x)) + \frac{d}{dx}(G(x))$.]

$= \frac{d}{dx}\left(\frac{1}{3}\exp(3x)\right) + \frac{d}{dx}\left(-\frac{1}{6}\cos(6x)\right)$

$= \exp(3x) + \sin(6x)$.

OR $\int \left(\exp(3x) + \sin(6x)\right) dx = \int \exp(3x)\, dx + \int \sin(6x)\, dx$

$= \frac{1}{3}\exp(3x) - \frac{1}{6}\cos(6x) + c$

[only one arbitrary constant needed in answer]

▶ What is $\int 5\cos(x)\, dx$?

From table:

$\cos(x)$ has an integral $\sin(x)$.

Guess: **Check:**   [Constant Multiple Rule]

$5\sin(x)$ $\frac{d}{dx}(5\sin(x)) = 5\frac{d}{dx}(\sin(x)) = 5\cos(x)$.

OR $\int 5\cos(x)\, dx = 5\int \cos(x)\, dx$

$= 5\sin(x) + c$

['$+ c$' is just as correct as '$+ 5c$']

FRAME 12

Rules for integrals

▶ Sum rule: $\displaystyle\int (f(x) + g(x))\,dx = \int f(x)\,dx + \int g(x)\,dx.$

▶ Constant Multiple Rule: $\displaystyle\int (bf(x))\,dx = b\int f(x)\,dx.$ *a constant multiple can be taken outside the integration*

▶ Combined: $\displaystyle\int (af(x) + bg(x))\,dx = a\int f(x)\,dx + b\int g(x)\,dx.$

FRAME 13

Applying the rules and table for integrals

▶ $\displaystyle\int (x^2 + 3x)\,dx = \int \boxed{}\,dx + \boxed{}\int \boxed{}\,dx$

$\quad = \boxed{} + \boxed{} + c.$ *(using table)*

▶ $\displaystyle\int \left(\exp(-3x) + \exp(2x) + \cos\left(\frac{x}{4}\right) \right) dx$

$\quad = \displaystyle\int \boxed{}\,dx + \int \boxed{}\,dx + \int \boxed{}\,dx$

$\quad = \boxed{} + \boxed{} + \boxed{} + c.$

▶ $\displaystyle\int \sqrt{x}\,dx = \int x^{\boxed{}}\,dx = \boxed{} + c.$

▶ $\displaystyle\int \left(9x^{-1/2} + 5x^{3/4} - 2x + \frac{1}{x} \right) dx \quad (x > 0)$ *combination of four integrals*

$\quad = \boxed{}$

$\quad = \boxed{}.$

▶ $\displaystyle\int x\left(x^3 + 2x^{-2/3} - \frac{1}{x} \right) dx$

$\quad = \displaystyle\int \left(\boxed{} \right) dx$ *multiplying out bracket*

$\quad = \boxed{}$

$\quad = \boxed{}$

In Frame 10 above, you derived a table of integrals, which is reproduced as Table 1.1 below.

Table 1.1

In each case, c is an arbitrary constant.

$f(x)$	$\int f(x)\,dx$
a (a constant)	$ax + c$
x^n $(n \neq -1)$	$\dfrac{x^{n+1}}{n+1} + c$
$\dfrac{1}{x}$ $(x > 0)$	$\ln x + c$
$\exp(ax)$	$\dfrac{1}{a}\exp(ax) + c$
$\cos(ax)$	$\dfrac{1}{a}\sin(ax) + c$
$\sin(ax)$	$-\dfrac{1}{a}\cos(ax) + c$

[handwritten note: raise the power by one divide by the new power + c]

Note that $\exp(ax)$ can be written also as e^{ax}. The constant a here can take any non-zero value.

In Frame 12, you obtained the **Sum Rule** for integrals,

$$\int (f(x) + g(x))dx = \int f(x)\,dx + \int g(x)\,dx, \tag{1.2}$$

and the **Constant Multiple Rule** for integrals,

$$\int k f(x)\,dx = k \int f(x)\,dx, \tag{1.3}$$

where k is any constant. It was noted that these can be combined into the single rule

$$\int (af(x) + bg(x))dx = a \int f(x)\,dx + b \int g(x)\,dx, \tag{1.4}$$

where a and b are any constants.

The following activities will give you further practice in the technique of applying these rules.

Activity 1.4   Applying the table and rules

Find each of the following indefinite integrals, using the results from Table 1.1 or the rules for integration stated in equations (1.2)–(1.4), as appropriate.

(a) $\displaystyle \int \left(x + 2x^2 \right) dx$

(b) $\displaystyle \int \left(\frac{1}{x} + \exp(2x) \right) dx$ (where $x > 0$)

(c) $\displaystyle \int (a\sin(\omega t) + b\cos(\omega t))\,dt$ (where a, b and ω are constants)

(d) $\displaystyle \int \left(x^{5/3} + x^{-1/2} + \exp(-2x) \right) dx$

(e) $\displaystyle \int (x+1)^2\,dx$ (*Hint:* First expand $(x+1)^2$ into a polynomial in x.)

Comment

Solutions are given on page 72.

Activity 1.5   Integrating two new functions

The functions cosh and sinh (known as the *hyperbolic cosine* and *hyperbolic sine*, respectively) are defined by

$$\cosh x = \frac{\exp(x) + \exp(-x)}{2} \quad \text{and} \quad \sinh x = \frac{\exp(x) - \exp(-x)}{2}.$$

Find each of the indefinite integrals

$$\int \cosh x \, dx \quad \text{and} \quad \int \sinh x \, dx.$$

Comment

Solutions are given on page 72.

Activity 1.6   Integrating the squares of cos and sin

From the two trigonometric formulas

$$\cos(2x) = \cos^2 x - \sin^2 x \quad \text{and} \quad \cos^2 x + \sin^2 x = 1,$$

it can be deduced that

$$\cos(2x) = 2\cos^2 x - 1,$$

and that

$$\cos(2x) = 1 - 2\sin^2 x.$$

By manipulating these last two formulas, find each of the following indefinite integrals.

(a) $\displaystyle\int \cos^2 x \, dx$ (b) $\displaystyle\int \sin^2 x \, dx$

Comment

Solutions are given on page 72.

Summary of Section 1

In this section, integration has been introduced as the 'undoing' of or inverse process to differentiation, and a number of integrals have been obtained.

◇   If $F(x)$ is any function whose derivative is $f(x)$, then $F(x) + c$ is another such function, for any value of the constant c. The *indefinite integral* of the function $f(x)$ is

$$\int f(x) \, dx = F(x) + c,$$

where c is an arbitrary constant. Any function such as $F(x)$ is referred to as *an* integral of $f(x)$. The process of finding the indefinite (or an) integral is called *integration*.

◇   The integrals of some commonly-occurring functions appear in Table 1.1 on page 20. In MST121 you will be expected to integrate any of these functions 'by hand', that is, without recourse to Mathcad.

◇   Further integrals may be found using the *Constant Multiple Rule* and *Sum Rule* for integrals; see equations (1.2)–(1.4).

Exercise for Section 1

Exercise 1.1

Find each of the following indefinite integrals, using the results from Table 1.1 or the rules for integration stated in equations (1.2)–(1.4), as appropriate.

(a) $\displaystyle\int t\sqrt{t}\,dt$ (b) $\displaystyle\int\left(\frac{3}{y^4}+5\sin(5y)\right)dy$ (c) $\displaystyle\int 2\cos\left(\frac{s}{7}\right)ds$

(d) $\displaystyle\int\left(\frac{3}{v}+\exp(3v)\right)dv$ (where $v>0$)   (e) $\displaystyle\int\exp(1+2x)\,dx$

2 Integration with Mathcad

To study this section, you will need access to your computer. Note that there are no Mathcad files associated with this section.

In the previous section integration was introduced, and you saw how to obtain the indefinite integrals of functions in a range of simple cases. By the end of the section, you were able to apply the results from Table 1.1 on page 20, together with the Sum and Constant Multiple Rules, in order to calculate certain integrals.

We have pointed out that integration is in effect the inverse process of differentiation. In Chapter C1, you saw that Mathcad can be used to find derivatives, which may lead you to wonder whether there is an analogous facility within Mathcad for integration. There is indeed an integral operator in Mathcad, and its application is the subject of this section.

2.1 Integrating simpler functions

As with differentiation, you are expected in MST121 to be able to find the integrals of simpler functions 'by hand', using the rules and table referred to above, while Mathcad can be applied for more complicated functions. However, in order to introduce the basics of integration using Mathcad, and to give you some confidence that Mathcad provides the same answers as those obtained from hand calculations, we ask you to start by considering anew functions whose integrals you found in Subsection 1.2.

Refer to Computer Book C for the work in this subsection.

In your work during this subsection you should have gained confidence in the integration capabilities of Mathcad, while noting certain respects in which care must be taken with the results.

2.2 Integrating more complicated functions

We turn now to the integration of functions of a more complicated type than those considered so far. While integration 'by hand' is not developed in this course to the point where it can be used to tackle these integrals, the range of functions which Mathcad can integrate is more extensive. Even so, as you will see, there are also functions (and not apparently very complicated ones) which are beyond the power of Mathcad to integrate.

Although we say that the functions whose integrals are sought here are 'more complicated' than those considered in Subsection 2.1, the form of these functions may not in fact be much less simple than the earlier cases. For example, the function $\tan x$ cannot be integrated by the approach used so far, but Mathcad provides its integral.

Refer to Computer Book C for the work in this subsection.

Your work with Mathcad in this subsection may have left you with a slight feeling of 'so what?'. The skill involved in using Mathcad for these more complicated integrals is largely confined to typing in correctly the algebraic expressions to be integrated, though it is useful to remember that even a Mathcad answer can be checked by applying the derivative operator to the outcome of an integral, to see whether this produces the original function.

Apart from undertaking such checks, you are taking on trust that Mathcad 'knows what it is doing'. This raises two important questions.

◇　How does Mathcad obtain its answers?

◇　How can we be sure (other than by constant checking, and even that involves another Mathcad operation) that it always gives a correct answer?

These questions are beyond the scope of MST121, but you can expect to see them considered if you take your mathematical studies further. This will entail, among other things, an extension to your ability to integrate 'by hand'.

Summary of Section 2

In this section you have seen how to use Mathcad in order to integrate a variety of functions.

You can use Mathcad to integrate simple functions as well as some more complicated ones. However, you are expected in MST121 to be able to integrate 'by hand' those functions which appear in Table 1.1. You will also be expected to apply the Constant Multiple Rule and Sum Rule for integrals where appropriate.

3 Differential equations and applications

Most of the mathematical models developed earlier in this course featured a direct relationship between the main variables. In this section you will study models where the initial connection between the variables is indirect, involving a *derivative*, and the resulting equation is called a *differential equation*. It is not possible in a single section to provide more than a brief introduction to what is a big subject, but the basics presented here should prove useful.

Differential equations are used frequently in mathematical modelling. You will see in a few instances how such equations arise in modelling real-life problems, and how integration can be used to find solutions to these equations.

You have previously come across one important class of problems for which the initial relationship between the variables is indirect. In Chapter A1, sequences were considered which satisfied a recurrence relation. In order to obtain a single sequence, the starting value had to be specified as well as the recurrence relation, to give a recurrence system. It was then possible in some cases to solve the recurrence system, by writing a rule for members of the sequence in closed form.

The programme for differential equations is similar to that for recurrence relations, though now we are dealing with continuous mathematics (and models) rather than the discrete variety. We are interested in functions which satisfy differential equations. In order to obtain a single function, we need to specify a starting value (or *initial condition*), to give an *initial-value problem*. It is then possible in some cases to solve such a problem and obtain an explicit formula for the rule of the function.

3.1 General and particular solutions

In Example 1.1 on page 9, we modelled the motion of a bungee jumper in free fall under gravity, in the time interval before the elastic rope tied to the jumper became taut. We argued that, since the acceleration of the falling jumper (in $\mathrm{m\,s^{-2}}$) is

$$\frac{dv}{dt} = 9.8, \tag{3.1}$$

then the velocity v of the jumper (in $\mathrm{m\,s^{-1}}$) is

$$v = 9.8t + c,$$

for some value of the constant c, where t denotes the time in seconds.

Following Example 1.1, we introduced the terminology and notation for indefinite integrals. In terms of these, the step just described can be recognised as finding the indefinite integral of the expression given for dv/dt. That is, if equation (3.1) holds, then we have

$$v = \int 9.8 \, dt$$
$$= 9.8t + c,$$

where c is an arbitrary constant.

Equation (3.1) is a simple example of a differential equation. More generally, a **differential equation** is an equation which features one or more derivatives. This description covers many possibilities. For example, each of the following is a differential equation:

$$\frac{dv}{dt} = \cos t; \qquad \frac{dP}{dt} = P;$$

$$\frac{d^2 s}{dx^2} = \exp x; \qquad \frac{d^2 y}{dx^2} + 3\frac{dy}{dx} - 2y = \sin(3x).$$

The first two of these equations are called *first-order* differential equations, because they include only a first derivative. The third and fourth equations are called *second-order* differential equations, because they feature a second derivative, but no third or higher derivatives. In this course, we consider only first-order differential equations. The second equation above will be analysed in Subsection 3.3, but before that we concentrate on differential equations of the form

$$\frac{dv}{dt} = f(t), \tag{3.2}$$

where f is a given function. The first of the four differential equations above is of this form, with $f(t) = \cos t$. So also is equation (3.1), with $f(t) = 9.8$. You should be able to recognise when an equation is of the form (3.2) even if different variable names are used. For example, the equation

$$\frac{dy}{dx} = f(x)$$

is of the same form, which in general can be described as

$$\frac{d(\text{dependent variable})}{d(\text{independent variable})} = f(\text{independent variable}).$$

We concentrate initially on equations of this type because they are precisely the differential equations for which a direct application of integration will provide solutions. If equation (3.2) holds, then we have

$$v = \int f(t)\, dt$$
$$= F(t) + c,$$

where c is an arbitrary constant and $F(t)$ is an integral of $f(t)$. (For the falling bungee jumper, we had $F(t) = 9.8t$.)

The expression $F(t) + c$ here is called the **general solution** of the differential equation (3.2). The general solution features an arbitrary constant, and describes all possible solutions of the differential equation. These properties apply also to differential equations other than the directly integrable type which we are currently considering.

Activity 3.1   Finding general solutions

Find the general solution of each of the following differential equations.

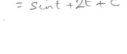

(a) $\dfrac{dP}{dt} = \cos t + 2$ (b) $\dfrac{dy}{dx} = \exp(4x) + \exp(-4x)$

(c) $\dfrac{dz}{du} = 3\sin(\omega u)$ (where ω is a constant)

Comment

Solutions are given on page 72.

Margin notes:

Second derivatives were introduced in Chapter C1 Subsection 4.2.

$P = \int(\cos t + 2)\,dt$

$= \sin t + 2t + c$

As stated above, the general solution of a differential equation is an expression which includes all possible solutions, any one of which is called a **particular solution**. In order to obtain a particular solution, it is necessary to specify a particular value for the arbitrary constant in the general solution, and this is often achieved by applying an **initial condition**, that is, a value of the dependent variable for some starting value of the independent variable. In a mathematical model, the initial condition arises from the particular circumstances of the situation being modelled.

For the bungee jumper in Example 1.1, for whom the general solution of the differential equation for the velocity v was

$$v = 9.8t + c,$$

we applied the initial condition that $v = 3$ when $t = 0$, corresponding to the information that the initial velocity of the jumper was 3 ms^{-1} downwards. This allowed us to deduce that $c = 3$, and hence that the particular solution of the differential equation corresponding to the given circumstances was

$$v = 9.8t + 3.$$

Which stages of the modelling cycle were revisited in Example 1.1?

Activity 3.2   Position of the bungee jumper

The last equation can be viewed as a differential equation for the position s m of the bungee jumper below the point of jump, since the velocity and position are related by $v = ds/dt$.

Can you locate this activity in the modelling cycle?

(a) Find the general solution of the differential equation

$$\frac{ds}{dt} = 9.8t + 3.$$

[handwritten] $S = \int 9.8t + 3 = \dfrac{9.8t^2}{2} + 3t = 4.9t^2 + 3t + c$

(b) The jump starts from $s = 0$ at time $t = 0$. Use this information to obtain the particular solution of the differential equation in part (a) which gives the position of the bungee jumper while in free fall, as a function of time. How far has the jumper fallen after 2 seconds?

[handwritten] use the initial condition to find the value of c
if $s = 0, t = 0$
then $c = 0$
so particular solution is
$s = 4.9t^2 + 3t$

Comment

Solutions are given on page 73.

[handwritten] if $t = 2$
$s = 4.9 \times 4 + 6$
$= 25.6$ m

The combination of a differential equation and an initial condition is called an **initial-value problem**. Thus, in the context of the bungee jumper, you have seen that the solution of the initial-value problem

$$\frac{dv}{dt} = 9.8, \quad v = 3 \text{ when } t = 0,$$

is $v = 9.8t + 3$, and that the solution of the initial-value problem

$$\frac{ds}{dt} = 9.8t + 3, \quad s = 0 \text{ when } t = 0,$$

is $s = 4.9t^2 + 3t$.

It is common in applied mathematics to allow symbols such as v and s above to 'do double duty', standing both for variables and for functions which relate variables. If these symbols stand for functions, then we may write the two initial-value problems respectively as

$$v'(t) = 9.8, \quad v(0) = 3,$$

and as

$$s'(t) = 9.8t + 3, \quad s(0) = 0.$$

This notation gives the initial condition in a more concise form. The use of the same symbol to denote both variable and function does not usually cause confusion, because the context determines which of the two possibilities is intended.

Activity 3.3 Solving initial-value problems

Using your answers to Activity 3.1, solve each of the following initial-value problems.

(a) $\dfrac{dP}{dt} = \cos t + 2, \quad P = 4$ when $t = 0$

(b) $\dfrac{dy}{dx} = \exp(4x) + \exp(-4x), \quad y = -1$ when $x = 0$

(c) $z'(u) = 3\sin(\omega u), \quad z(0) = \omega^{-1} \quad$ (where ω is a constant)

Comment

Solutions are given on page 73.

Handwritten annotation:

General solution is
$P = \int \cos t + 2 \, dt$
$\Rightarrow P = \sin t + 2t + C$
From initial condition
when $P = 4, \ t = 0$
$\quad C = 4$
So solution of initial-value
problem is
$\quad P = \sin t + 2t + 4$

The process of solving differential equations depends upon integration. However, you saw in Subsection 2.2 some functions for which integration cannot produce a simple answer, that is, an answer expressible as an algebraic formula involving the standard functions. The same limitation therefore applies to solving differential equations. In such cases, where an initial condition is given, alternative methods exist for finding an approximate numerical solution to the initial-value problem. You will see an indication of how such approximate solutions can be obtained later in the chapter.

Activity 3.4 Differential equations and modelling

Summarise on Learning File Sheet 2 the procedure for solving a differential equation (of the type considered above) in your own words. What is a general solution? What is a particular solution? What is an initial condition? How do you determine the arbitrary constant? Finally, consider some of the situations you have met which can be modelled by this kind of equation. Begin a list now and add to it as you come across new examples.

3.2 Motion with constant acceleration

Most of this subsection is concerned with a practical problem which is of importance to any driver of a vehicle. Firstly, however, we shall tidy up and generalise the mathematics which you saw used to find the velocity and position functions of the bungee jumper, starting from the jumper's acceleration. This generalisation will then be put to use in setting up the model which follows.

Suppose that an object moves along a straight line, on which a positive direction of motion and reference point (origin) have been chosen. Suppose also that the object has an acceleration a m s^{-2} which remains *constant* throughout the motion.

The motion of the bungee jumper while in free fall is one example of such a motion, with $a = 9.8$. However, in what follows, the value of a need not necessarily be regarded as positive. If a is negative then, as long as the object is moving in the positive direction, it is *decelerating*.

The acceleration is the derivative of the velocity, v m s^{-1}, and so we have

$$\frac{dv}{dt} = a \quad \text{(constant)}.$$

For a reminder of the various possibilities for the signs of velocity and acceleration of the object, see Example 4.1 in Chapter C1 Subsection 4.2.

Integration gives

$$v = \int a\, dt = at + c,$$

where c is an arbitrary constant. Now c is the value of v when $t = 0$, and in recognition of this, we write it as the constant v_0, to obtain

$$v = at + v_0. \tag{3.3}$$

When v represents the velocity *function*, we may write

$$v(0) = v_0.$$

The velocity is the derivative of the displacement or position, s m, and so we have

$$\frac{ds}{dt} = at + v_0.$$

Integration gives

$$s = \int (at + v_0)\, dt = \tfrac{1}{2}at^2 + v_0 t + c,$$

where c is an arbitrary constant. Here c is the value of s when $t = 0$, and in recognition of this, we write it as the constant s_0, to obtain

$$s = \tfrac{1}{2}at^2 + v_0 t + s_0. \tag{3.4}$$

When s represents the position *function*, we may write

$$s(0) = s_0.$$

The two equations (3.3) and (3.4) give expressions for the velocity and position of any motion in one dimension with constant acceleration.

Note that in the special case when the object starts from the chosen origin with zero velocity, that is, when $s_0 = v_0 = 0$, equations (3.3) and (3.4) reduce to

$$v = at \quad \text{and} \quad s = \tfrac{1}{2}at^2.$$

With $a = g = 9.8$ m s^{-2}, these are the formulas which appeared in the 'standard model' for falling objects considered in Chapter C1 Subsection 4.3. Equations (3.3) and (3.4) represent a generalisation of the earlier model to any one-dimensional motion with constant acceleration.

We move next to the practical problem mentioned at the start of the subsection, for which the mathematical results just derived will assist in obtaining a solution.

How far before you can stop?

When driving a car, you need to be aware of the distance ahead within which you can come safely to a halt by braking. For example, if the next vehicle ahead of you on the road is stationary, while you are moving, then you must start to brake before you become too close to the other vehicle, in order to avoid a collision.

This raises the question of just what is the minimum stopping distance required for safety purposes, and mathematical modelling can be brought to bear on this question. The results of any model should, of course, be treated cautiously, given the possible consequences of error. A safety margin can be added if such results are to be published or otherwise put into practice.

Specify purpose

In order to start modelling, we need to specify the purpose of the model. The purpose in this case is to obtain the minimum distance within which a car can be brought to a halt.

However, a little reflection shows that this statement is not sufficiently precise. There is no single distance which can be regarded as a satisfactory answer to the problem, since a car which is initially travelling slowly can be stopped safely on a shorter stretch of road than would be needed if it were travelling faster. In other words, the stopping distance which we seek will depend upon the initial velocity of the car, and this fact should be recognised in our specification of the purpose of the model:

◇   to obtain the minimum distance within which a car can be brought to a halt, in terms of its initial velocity.

Create model

In order to create a mathematical model to address this problem, we make some simplifying assumptions, as follows.

◇   The car travels in a horizontal straight line while braking. (Thus the road is flat and straight, and motion from one lane to another is not attempted.)

◇   The car does not skid when the brakes are applied.

◇   The road is dry, and the car and tyres are in good condition.

◇   The acceleration of the car while braking (which is in fact a deceleration) is constant.

From the first and last of these assumptions, it will be possible to apply equations (3.3) and (3.4) to this situation. We choose the positive direction of motion to be that in which the car is moving, with the origin for position at the point where the brakes are first applied. While braking occurs, the following quantities are relevant:

◇ t, the time since the brakes were first applied, in seconds;

◇ s, the position of the car at time t, in metres;

◇ v, the velocity of the car at time t, in $\mathrm{m\,s}^{-1}$;

◇ a, the constant acceleration of the car, in $\mathrm{m\,s}^{-2}$.

Since the car decelerates, while v is positive for the chosen direction of motion, the value of a is negative.

We shall also use subscripts, where appropriate, to denote the values of t, s and v at the two ends of the decelerating motion, with the subscript 0 at the start and the subscript 1 where the motion stops. All of the important quantities are included on the following diagram.

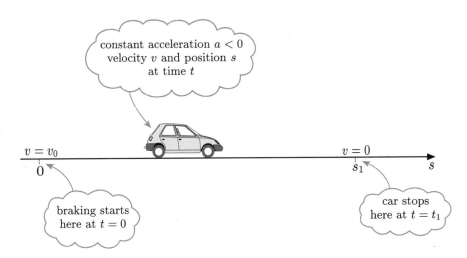

Figure 3.1

The notation has been chosen to agree with that used in deriving equations (3.3) and (3.4), so these may now be referred to as stated.

$$v = at + v_0 \qquad (3.3)$$
$$s = \tfrac{1}{2}at^2 + v_0 t + s_0 \qquad (3.4)$$

From the choice of origin for the motion, we have

$$s_0 = 0. \qquad (3.5)$$

At the instant when the car comes to a halt, we have

$$v = 0 \quad \text{and} \quad s = s_1 \quad \text{when } t = t_1. \qquad (3.6)$$

This completes the formulation of the mathematical model. The purpose of the model was stated to be

to obtain the minimum distance within which a car can be brought to a halt, in terms of its initial velocity.

Leaving aside the 'minimum' aspect for the moment, the mathematical problem which needs to be solved in line with this purpose is:

◇   to find s_1 in terms of v_0.

On using equations (3.5) and (3.6) to substitute in equations (3.3) and (3.4), we obtain

$$0 = at_1 + v_0,$$
$$s_1 = \tfrac{1}{2}at_1^2 + v_0 t_1.$$

We can now relate s_1 to v_0 by eliminating the unknown time t_1 between these two equations. The first equation gives

$$t_1 = -\frac{v_0}{a},$$

so that the second equation provides

$$s_1 = \tfrac{1}{2}a\left(-\frac{v_0}{a}\right)^2 + v_0\left(-\frac{v_0}{a}\right)$$
$$= \frac{v_0^2}{2a} - \frac{v_0^2}{a} = -\frac{v_0^2}{2a}.$$

We have reached the equation

$$s_1 = -\frac{v_0^2}{2a}, \qquad (3.7)$$

which relates the stopping distance s_1 to the initial velocity v_0 as required, with the constant acceleration a appearing as a parameter in the equation.

Remember that $a < 0$. This explains the presence of the minus sign here and in the equation for t_1 above.

31

At this stage of the mathematical modelling cycle, we need to interpret the results. This can be carried out on both a qualitative and quantitative level. For example, one way of interpreting equation (3.7) qualitatively is to sketch the graph of s_1 against v_0 for a fixed value of a, as shown in Figure 3.2 below.

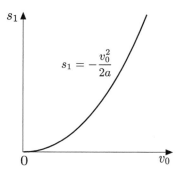

$$s_1 = -\frac{v_0^2}{2a}$$

Figure 3.2

This illustrates the fact that the stopping distance increases as the square of the initial velocity, which is larger than a linear rate of increase. Thus the effect of doubling the initial velocity, for a given braking force, is to increase the stopping distance fourfold.

It is also clear from equation (3.7) that, for a fixed initial velocity, the stopping distance is inversely proportional to the magnitude of the acceleration, so that stopping distance is minimised by applying the greatest possible braking force. This prediction seems very reasonable!

For a quantitative interpretation, we need to insert some numerical value for the acceleration a, and suitable data are available. Most cars with brakes in good condition (as assumed earlier) can achieve a braking force corresponding to $a = -8$ m s^{-2}, though the minimum requirement for passing the MOT test corresponds to only $a = -5$ m s^{-2}. The Highway Code gives a table of stopping distances which are based on an acceleration of about $a = -6.56$ m s^{-2}.

Taking this last figure for illustrative purposes, it is possible to evaluate the stopping distance s_1, from equation (3.7), for any desired value of the initial velocity v_0. For example,

$$\text{if } v_0 = 30, \text{ then } s_1 = \frac{30^2}{2 \times 6.56} \simeq 69,$$

30 m s^{-1} is about 67 mph.

so the stopping distance for an initial velocity of 30 m s^{-1} is predicted to be about 69 metres.

Having interpreted the results, we reach the modelling stage of evaluating the outcome. We pointed out at the start that the results of such a model should be interpreted with caution, and the need for this is emphasised by the variation in values which could be chosen for the acceleration a. The Highway Code value seems quite conservative when compared with the figure quoted for brakes in good condition, but in either case one might expect a significant reduction in braking performance in wet conditions. These conditions would also increase the chances of skidding.

The Highway Code model for stopping distances includes an important element which we have not yet considered, and that is the reaction time of the driver. There is an appreciable time lag between the first realisation that braking is required and the actual application of the brakes, and an improved model for the stopping distance needs to take this into account.

If the driver takes r seconds to react, then he or she will have travelled a distance rv_0 metres before the brakes are applied. Adding this to the right-hand side of equation (3.7) gives the amended model

$$s_1 = rv_0 - \frac{v_0^2}{2a},$$

for the stopping distance. The Highway Code assumes a reaction time of about 0.7 seconds. For the initial velocity 30 m s^{-1} considered before, the effect of including this reaction time is to increase the predicted overall stopping distance from 69 to 90 metres.

That concludes our mathematical modelling for the problem of predicting safe stopping distances. However, there is one mathematical feature encountered above which is worth expanding upon. In order to relate s_1 to v_0, we eliminated the time t_1 between two equations. This step can be generalised, and the outcome is particularly useful in cases where we wish to relate velocity and position without explicitly involving the time. You are invited to derive the general result in the next Activity.

Activity 3.5   No time!

An object moving along a straight line with constant acceleration a satisfies the two equations

$$v = at + v_0, \tag{3.3}$$
$$s = \tfrac{1}{2}at^2 + v_0 t + s_0. \tag{3.4}$$

By eliminating the time t between these two equations, obtain a direct relationship between the position s and velocity v of the object.

Comment

A solution is given on page 73.

The result which you have just obtained states that the quantity

$$2as - v^2$$

remains constant throughout the motion since, at any time, it is equal to its initial value $2as_0 - v_0^2$. This result ranks in importance alongside equations (3.3) and (3.4).

> **Motion with constant acceleration**
>
> The following formulas apply for the motion of an object along a straight line with constant acceleration a, if at time $t = 0$ the object has velocity v_0 and position s_0.
>
> ◇   The velocity v of the object is given by
>
> $$v = at + v_0. \tag{3.3}$$
>
> ◇   The position s of the object is given by
>
> $$s = \tfrac{1}{2}at^2 + v_0 t + s_0. \tag{3.4}$$
>
> ◇   The velocity and position of the object are related by the equation
>
> $$2as - v^2 = 2as_0 - v_0^2. \tag{3.8}$$

A direct application of equation (3.8) would have shortened our working in setting up and solving the mathematical problem for car stopping distances. Since $s_0 = 0$, and $s = s_1$ when $v = 0$, equation (3.8) gives

$$s_1 = -\frac{v_0^2}{2a} \qquad (3.7)$$

once more.

Equation (3.8) is particularly useful for models involving constant acceleration in which the main variables are position and velocity. If time appears explicitly in the problem, then one of equations (3.3) or (3.4) must be applied.

Example 3.1   Dropping a stone

The height of the Eiffel Tower is 300 metres. Suppose that a stone is dropped from rest at the top of the tower.

(a) Ignoring air resistance, estimate the speed of the stone when it hits the ground.

(b) How long does the stone take to reach the ground?

Solution

(a) Choose the positive direction to be vertically downwards, with the origin at the top of the tower. Then, since air resistance is ignored, the stone has the constant acceleration $a = g = 9.8 \text{ m s}^{-2}$. The stone is released from rest, that is, with zero velocity, at the origin, so we have $v_0 = s_0 = 0$. Equation (3.8) therefore gives

$$2 \times 9.8s - v^2 = 0$$

for the motion of the dropping stone. The stone hits the ground at $s = 300$, at which point its speed is

$$v = \sqrt{2 \times 9.8 \times 300} \simeq 76.7 \text{ m s}^{-1}.$$

(b) To find the value of t when the stone hits the ground, we need to use either equation (3.3) or equation (3.4), and the first of these is the simpler to apply. For the value of v just calculated, we have

$$t = \frac{v - v_0}{a}$$
$$= \frac{\sqrt{2 \times 9.8 \times 300} - 0}{9.8} \simeq 7.8 \text{ seconds.}$$

Activity 3.6   Braking again

An aircraft touches down with a speed of 70 m s^{-1} at the end of a runway whose length is 550 m. The pilot is required to reduce the speed of the aircraft to at most 5 m s^{-1}, prior to taxiing off the runway at its other end.

(a) Calculate the minimum magnitude of acceleration (deceleration) during braking which will achieve this requirement.

(b) When braking with this deceleration, how long does it take the aircraft to travel the length of the runway?

Comment

Solutions are given on page 73.

3.3 Population growth and radioactive decay

In Subsection 3.1 we considered differential equations of the form

$$\frac{dv}{dt} = f(t), \qquad\qquad (3.2)$$

in which the right-hand side is a function of the independent variable. We now turn to a class of differential equations for which the right-hand side is proportional to the dependent variable, that is, equations of the form

$$\frac{dP}{dt} = kP, \qquad\qquad (3.9)$$

where k is a constant. As before, you should be able to recognise when an equation is of this form even if different names are used for the variables. For example, the equations

$$\frac{dy}{dx} = ky \quad \text{and} \quad \frac{dm}{dt} = km$$

are both of the same form as equation (3.9).

Equations of this type occur frequently in mathematical models, since they embody the idea that an instantaneous rate of change of a quantity is proportional to the current amount or value of the quantity. Some situations which can be modelled in this way are the size of a population, the proportion of a radioactive substance present in an object, the amount of money in a savings account, or the temperature of a cup of tea above that of its surroundings.

For a cup of tea, for example, the temperature falls rapidly at first, while the tea is hot, but the rate of cooling diminishes as the temperature becomes closer to that of the surrounding air. On the other hand, a colony of bacteria may grow slowly while the population size is small, but expand at a dramatic rate when the numbers are larger. The phrase 'exponential increase' is often used to describe this sort of phenomenon, and you will see shortly that this is an apt description. If the proportionality constant k is positive, then the differential equation (3.9) represents *exponential growth*, whereas if k is negative (as would be the case for the tea temperature), then it describes *exponential decay*.

A continuous model for population growth

You have already seen earlier in the course some mathematical models for the way in which population size alters with time. This topic was introduced in Chapter A2 and developed further in Chapter B2. However, these models all had the property that they predicted the population size only at discrete intervals of time (typically at annual intervals). The aim here is to consider a model which describes a population at *any* instant of time, on a continuously changing basis. In practice, of course, populations are made up of individuals, and so the size of a population can take only integer values and does not change continuously. However, if the population size is large, then its behaviour may be approximated satisfactorily by a continuous function, and continuous models for populations are therefore of value.

The discrete models discussed earlier in the course may be considered most appropriate where the behaviour of the population has a naturally periodic aspect, as would be the case where all births take place in an annual breeding season. For populations whose growth is not determined by such a cyclical pattern, either a continuous or discrete model may be adopted.

If P represents the size of a population at time t, then the instantaneous rate of change of the population is given by the derivative dP/dt. This rate of change can be analysed as in the previous models in terms of the rates at which 'joiners' and 'leavers' affect the population. If migration is not an important factor, then dP/dt is essentially the instantaneous birth rate minus the instantaneous death rate, and a simple modelling assumption is that each of these is proportional to the current population size. We then have

$$\frac{dP}{dt} = bP - dP,$$

where bP and dP are the birth and death rates, respectively, and b, d are constants of proportionality. This can be written as

$$\frac{dP}{dt} = (b - d)P = kP,$$

Note that, since we are modelling a population, we require $P \geq 0$ at all times.

where $k = b - d$ is another constant. If $b > d$, that is, if the birth rate is greater than the death rate, then we have $k > 0$ and $dP/dt > 0$, in which case the population is increasing. If $b < d$ then $k < 0$, so that $dP/dt < 0$ and the population decreases. With $b = d$ we have $k = 0$, so $dP/dt = 0$ and the population remains at a constant size. The model for population change which we have arrived at is

$$\frac{dP}{dt} = kP, \tag{3.9}$$

and we now consider how this differential equation may be solved.

Solving the differential equation

The method of direct integration, which we used to find the general solution for equations of the form

$$\frac{dv}{dt} = f(t), \tag{3.2}$$

will not work in solving equation (3.9). We can indeed integrate both sides of equation (3.9) with respect to t, to obtain

$$P = k \int P \, dt.$$

At this point, however, we become stuck! The integral on the right-hand side cannot be evaluated unless P can be replaced by a function of t, but it is precisely that function whose form we seek.

In order to make progress, we may revert to the strategy adopted in Subsection 1.2 of 'guess and check'. You are invited to try this in the next Activity.

Activity 3.7   Finding solutions

(a) The equation

$$\frac{dP}{dt} = kP \tag{3.9}$$

general solution
is
$P = A \exp(kt)$

states that the derivative of P is proportional to P itself. By looking in the table of derivatives in Frame 3 of Subsection 1.2, identify a type of function which has this property.

(b) Write down one solution of equation (3.9).

(c) The general solution of this differential equation should feature an arbitrary constant.

(i) Show that adding '$+c$' to your answer to part (b) does *not* produce further solutions to the differential equation in this case.

(ii) Show that any constant multiple of your answer to part (b) *is* a solution to equation (3.9).

(d) What is the particular solution of equation (3.9) which satisfies the initial condition

$$P = P_0 \text{ when } t = 0?$$

Comment

(a) According to the table of derivatives, we have

$$\frac{d}{dx}(\exp(ax)) = a\exp(ax),$$

so exponential functions have the property stated.

(b) Choosing $a = k$, and replacing x by t, we obtain

$$\frac{d}{dt}(\exp(kt)) = k\exp(kt),$$

so

$$P = \exp(kt)$$

is one solution of equation (3.9).

(c) (i) If $P = \exp(kt) + c$, where c is a non-zero constant, then

$$\frac{dP}{dt} = \frac{d}{dt}(\exp(kt)) = k\exp(kt) \neq kP,$$

and hence $P = \exp(kt) + c$ is *not* a solution of equation (3.9).

(ii) If $P = A\exp(kt)$, where A is any constant, then

$$\frac{dP}{dt} = A\frac{d}{dt}(\exp(kt)) = Ak\exp(kt) = kP,$$

and hence $P = A\exp(kt)$ *is* a solution of equation (3.9).

In fact, $P = A\exp(kt)$, where A is an arbitrary constant, is the general solution of equation (3.9).

(d) If $P = A\exp(kt)$ then, on putting $t = 0$, we have $P_0 = A$. The particular solution required is therefore $P = P_0\exp(kt)$.

In this activity, you showed that the solution of the initial value-problem

$$\frac{dP}{dt} = kP, \quad P = P_0 \text{ when } t = 0,$$

is

$$P = P_0\exp(kt). \tag{3.10}$$

For obvious reasons, the equation $dP/dt = kP$ is called the *exponential model* for population change. Before considering some detailed applications of this model, note that the differential equation can also be written as

$$\frac{1}{P}\frac{dP}{dt} = k.$$

rate of popⁿ
growth per head
proportionate)
growth rate)

The expression on the left-hand side here is the rate of population change divided by the current population size, or the rate of change per head. This quantity is also called the *proportionate growth rate*, and the model which we have just constructed therefore describes any population for which the proportionate growth rate is a constant, k. Annual birth rates and death rates of actual populations are typically quoted as percentages or as so many per thousand, and if these are constant then they correspond to the constants of proportionality b and d used in deriving the differential equation (3.9), where $k = b - d$.

This re-expression of the differential equation also shows that the units of the proportionate growth rate k are time^{-1}, that is, s^{-1} if time is measured in seconds, year^{-1} if time is measured in years, and so on.

Example 3.2   Breeding bacteria

A colony of bacteria numbers 1000 at midday on 1 June, and its growth can be modelled by an exponential model with proportionate growth rate 1 per day.

(a) Express the population size as a function of time.

(b) What is the size of this population one day later, at midday on 2 June?

Solution

(a) We have $k = 1$ and $P_0 = 1000$, so the population size at time t days after midday on 1 June is

$$P = 1000 \exp(t).$$

(b) At midday on 2 June, the time in days is $t = 1$, and the number of bacteria has therefore reached

$$P = 1000 \exp(1) = 2720 \text{ (to 3 s.f.)}.$$

Activity 3.8   A human population

The population of a certain country is currently 10 million, and is increasing at 3% per year. Use the exponential model to predict what the population of the country will be in ten years time.

Comment

A solution is given on page 74.

The results of Activity 3.7 apply more widely than to the context of populations.

Activity 3.9   Finding particular solutions

(a) Find the particular solution of the differential equation

$$\frac{dy}{dx} = 2y$$

for which $y = 100$ when $x = 0$.

(b) Find the particular solution of the differential equation

$$\frac{dv}{dt} = -3v$$

for which $v = 15$ when $t = 0$.

Comment

Solutions are given on page 74.

Returning to the use of the equation

$$\frac{dP}{dt} = kP \tag{3.9}$$

as a model for populations, the form of solution

$$P = P_0 \exp(kt)$$

has an interesting consequence in terms of the factor by which the population size is multiplied over any fixed time interval. This relies on the fact that $\exp(kt)$ can also be written as e^{kt}. Hence the population at a fixed interval T after any time t is given by

$$P_0 \exp(k(t+T)) = P_0 e^{kt+kT} = P_0 e^{kT} e^{kt} = \exp(kT) P_0 \exp(kt).$$

This says that, in a time interval of duration T, the population is multiplied by the factor $\exp(kT)$, regardless of what the time was at the start of the interval.

Example 3.3 Doubling time

(a) Suppose that the behaviour of a certain population is described by the exponential model, with proportionate growth rate $k > 0$. Determine, in terms of k, the time which it takes for the population size to double. (This is known as the *doubling time* for the population.)

(b) Find the doubling time for the human population considered in Activity 3.8.

Solution

(a) From the text above the example, the doubling time T is given by

$$\exp(kT) = 2.$$

The value of T is found by taking the natural logarithm of both sides, and then dividing by k, which gives

$$T = \frac{\ln 2}{k}.$$

(b) For the population in Activity 3.8, the proportionate growth rate was $k = 0.03$ year^{-1}. The doubling time for this population is therefore

$$T = \frac{\ln 2}{0.03} \simeq 23.1 \text{ years.}$$

In some situations involving populations, it may be necessary to deduce the value of the proportionate growth rate from other information, as in the case below.

Activity 3.10   Insects

Suppose that the population of a species of insect within a certain habitat is described by the exponential model. Initially there are 50 insects and, after one day, there are 1000 insects.

(a) Find an expression for the population of insects as a function of time.

(b) What is the population size after 2 days?

(c) What is the doubling time for the population?

Comment

Solutions are given on page 74.

The exponential model for population growth matches reality quite well for a variety of populations, provided that the comparison is taken over a finite time interval. A deficiency of the model is that, with any positive value of k, it predicts an unlimited growth of the population. This is an impossibility, and in practice the model becomes unreliable at relatively high population levels. There is not space here for a discussion of why this is so, or of how the assumptions of the exponential model can be improved, but this issue was tackled in the discrete case in Chapter B2 Subsection 2.1, in moving from the 'geometric' to the logistic model.

However, note that, by altering the assumptions of the model in a similar way to that effected in the discrete case, we can formulate an improved continuous model (also called *logistic*) which features a slightly more complicated differential equation and avoids the prediction of unlimited growth.

All of the population examples considered above with the exponential model have featured positive values for the proportionate growth rate k, corresponding to increasing populations. The exponential model can also be applied to declining populations, for which the corresponding value of k is negative. However, rather than look at such cases, we shall introduce an alternative context for which the exponential model applies and the value of k is always negative.

A model for radioactive decay

As you may know, the nuclei of radioactive substances tend to disintegrate spontaneously, at a rate which varies according to the substance concerned. The effect is to reduce the amount of the radioactive substance present, and to alter the chemical composition of the object within which the substance resides.

Substantial experimental evidence suggests that the rate of decay of a radioactive substance is proportional to the amount of it which is present in an object. Consequently, the mass m of radioactive substance present at time t can be modelled by the equation

$$\frac{dm}{dt} = -\lambda m,$$

The symbol λ is the Greek letter lambda.

where λ is a positive constant.

This is of the same form as equation (3.9), with $k = -\lambda$, and so its solution is obtainable from equation (3.10) as

$$m = m_0 \exp(-\lambda t), \tag{3.11}$$

where m_0 is the value of m at $t = 0$.

The constant λ is called the *decay rate* or *transformation constant* of the radioactive substance. While the radioactivity of substances can be described in terms of their decay rates, it is usual to refer instead to another characteristic constant known as the *half-life* of the substance. This is defined analogously to the doubling time for a growing population. In fact, the half-life is the time which it takes for the mass of radioactive substance present to diminish to half of its original amount, so for a half-life T, we have from equation (3.11) that

decay rate
- See note in
Stop press 3 p 2

$$\tfrac{1}{2}m_0 = m_0 \exp(-\lambda T).$$

On cancelling the m_0 and taking logarithms, we obtain

$$\ln \tfrac{1}{2} = -\lambda T,$$

or

$$\lambda T = \ln 2.$$

This equation can be used to find either of λ or T from the other.

Radioactive substances have a very wide range of half-lives, from millions of years down to tiny fractions of a second.

Example 3.4   How much is left?

One isotope of silicon has a half-life of 2.62 hours. What proportion of an original quantity of this isotope will still be present after six hours?

Solution

For a half-life of 2.62 hours, the decay rate is

$$\lambda = \frac{\ln 2}{2.62} = 0.265 \text{ hour}^{-1}.$$

The mass m of isotope present at time t is therefore

$$m = m_0 \exp(-0.265t),$$

where m_0 is the amount present initially (at $t = 0$). After six hours, the proportion of the original amount remaining is

$$\frac{m}{m_0} = \exp(-0.265 \times 6) = 0.204,$$

so about 20% of the original amount of isotope remains.

One useful application of radioactivity is to the dating of archaeological finds. Carbon occurs naturally in two forms, carbon 12 and carbon 14. Chemically they are indistinguishable, but carbon 14 is radioactive and decays continually into nitrogen. In the 1950s, Willard F. Libby made the following discovery. In living tissue, carbon 14 is always being renewed, so that the proportion of carbon 14 present is constant. However, when an organism dies and is buried the carbon is no longer replenished, and the proportion of carbon 14 decreases with time as it decays.

Carbon 14 has a half-life of approximately 5570 years, so there are still appreciable amounts of it left in dead matter even after thousands of years. The quantity of carbon 14 in tissue can be estimated from a measurement of the radioactivity, while the total quantity of carbon can be estimated from chemical analysis. Libby's discovery thus forms the basis for a method of estimating when the organism died, which is known as the method of *carbon dating*.

Activity 3.11   How old?

The skeleton of an animal is found in an archaeological dig. Analysis produces the estimate that 15% of the original amount of carbon 14 is still present in the skeleton. Taking the half-life of carbon 14 as 5570 years, find the approximate age of the skeleton.

Comment

A solution is given on page 74.

Summary of Section 3

In this section, the topic of differential equations was introduced.

◇   A *differential equation* is an equation which features one or more derivatives. *First-order* differential equations feature only a first derivative. The *general solution* of a differential equation is an expression which describes all possible solutions of the equation. A first-order differential equation together with an *initial condition* (giving the value of the dependent variable for one value of the independent variable) makes up an *initial-value problem*, which specifies a *particular solution* of the differential equation.

◇   The general solution of the differential equation

$$\frac{dv}{dt} = f(t),$$

where $f(t)$ is a given function, is

$$v = \int f(t)\, dt$$
$$= F(t) + c,$$

where c is an arbitrary constant and $F(t)$ is an integral of $f(t)$.

◇   The following formulas apply for the motion of an object along a straight line with constant acceleration a, if at time $t = 0$ the object has velocity v_0 and position s_0.

(i)   The velocity v of the object is given by

$$v = at + v_0.$$

(ii)   The position s of the object is given by

$$s = \tfrac{1}{2}at^2 + v_0 t + s_0.$$

(iii) The velocity and position of the object are related by the equation

$$2as - v^2 = 2as_0 - v_0^2.$$

◇   The initial-value problem

$$\frac{dP}{dt} = kP, \quad P = P_0 \text{ when } t = 0,$$

where k is a constant, has solution

$$P = P_0 \exp(kt).$$

It can be used as a model for population growth (with P as the population size at time t), in which context the differential equation is called the *exponential model*. The constant k is the *proportionate growth rate* of the population, which (for $k > 0$) has a *doubling time T* given by

$$T = \frac{\ln 2}{k}.$$

◇   The same type of differential equation, written as

$$\frac{dm}{dt} = -\lambda m,$$

can be used to model the mass m of a substance decaying radioactively, at time t. The positive constant λ is called the *decay rate*. The solution is now

$$m = m_0 \exp(-\lambda t),$$

where m_0 is the mass of the substance present at time $t = 0$. The *half-life T* of the substance, which is the time taken for the mass of substance present to decrease by half, is given by

$$T = \frac{\ln 2}{\lambda}.$$

Exercises for Section 3

Exercise 3.1

Solve each of the following initial-value problems.

(a) $\dfrac{dy}{dx} = x^3 - 1, \quad y = 5$ when $x = 0$

(b) $v'(t) = 4\cos(2t) - 5\sin(3t), \quad v(0) = 1$

Exercise 3.2

A ball is projected vertically upwards with speed $25\,\mathrm{m\,s^{-1}}$. Its subsequent motion is to be modelled by ignoring air resistance and taking $g = 9.8\,\mathrm{m\,s^{-2}}$.

(a) What is the maximum height attained by the ball above its point of projection?

(b) How long does the ball take to return to the point of projection?

(c) At what times is the ball $20\,\mathrm{m}$ above its point of projection?

Exercise 3.3

The age of an ancient piece of wood, uncovered during an archaeological dig, is to be estimated using carbon dating. Analysis of a sample of the wood shows that the proportion of the original carbon 14 present is 0.6. Taking the half-life of carbon 14 as 5570 years, estimate the age of the piece of wood.

4 Definite integrals, areas and summations

 You will need access to your computer, together with the disk with the Mathcad file for this chapter and Computer Book C, in order to study Subsection 4.3.

You have seen that integration is the 'undoing' of differentiation, and that it may therefore be put to use in solving differential equations. In this section we link what has been done to another aspect of integration, which on the face of it is very different from the first. This involves seeing integration as a process related to the summation of a number of terms, in the limit as that number becomes large. The link between this and our original view of integration is of considerable mathematical importance, and is also important from a modelling point of view.

4.1 Areas under graphs and the definite integral

It is often necessary in a practical situation to estimate the extent of an area. For example, building regulations refer to the ground area to be occupied by a piece of land or a building, so that the extent of such areas must be apparent from a building plan. When a surface is to be painted, the painter needs to know how much paint is required to do the job, and in essence this depends on finding the area of the surface.

Paint manufacturers state on their cans what area can be covered by a given volume of the paint.

Sometimes area on a diagram is used to represent another type of physical quantity. For example, in Block D you will see cases where areas bounded above by the graph of a function represent the probabilities of certain events taking place.

When areas are bounded by segments of straight lines, their calculation is relatively simple. All such calculations depend ultimately on the formula for the area of a rectangle, which is bh for a rectangle with base b and height h. The area of a triangle can be seen to be half that of an associated rectangle. If the triangle has base b and height h, then its area is $\frac{1}{2}bh$. More general areas which are bounded by straight lines can be regarded as being made up of a number of triangular areas.

This leaves the question of how to calculate areas when at least part of the boundary is curved. An example is shown in Figure 4.1(a) below, where the area of interest is bounded by straight lines on three sides, but by the graph of a non-linear function f on the fourth. This is referred to as the *area under the graph of $f(x)$ from $x = a$ to $x = b$.*

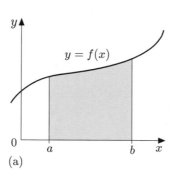
(a)

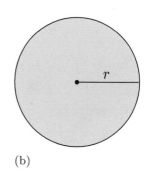
(b)

Figure 4.1

Another example, shown in Figure 4.1(b), is the area of a circle. No doubt you are aware that the area of a circle of radius r is πr^2, but where does this formula come from? You will see an answer to this question shortly.

Our approach in this subsection is as follows. Firstly you are asked to find the areas of a couple of regions which are made up of rectangles and triangles, but for which an application of integration can be shown to give the same answer. Building on these suggestive results, we argue that integration provides a means of calculating areas of the type shown in Figure 4.1(a), for any continuous function f. Then we look at the application of this integration approach in a variety of cases where f is a non-linear function.

Activity 4.1   Area of a rectangle

(a) What is the area under the graph of the function $f(x) = 3$, which is bounded also by the x-axis and by the lines $x = 0$ and $x = 5$ (see Figure 4.2)?

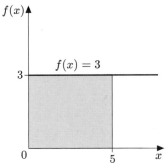

Figure 4.2

(b) Choose an integral $F(x)$ of the function given in part (a), and evaluate $F(5) - F(0)$. What do you notice?

Comment

Solutions are given on page 74.

Activity 4.2   Area of a trapezium

(a) What is the area under the graph of the function $f(x) = 2x + 3$, which is bounded also by the x-axis and by the lines $x = -1$ and $x = 2$ (see Figure 4.3)?

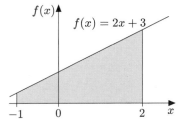

Figure 4.3

(b) Choose an integral $F(x)$ of the function given in part (a), and evaluate $F(2) - F(-1)$. What do you notice?

Comment

Solutions are given on page 75.

On the basis of the results in these two activities, we can surmise that the following might be true.

Hypothesis

Suppose that $f(x)$ is a continuous function which takes no negative values for $a \leq x \leq b$ (so that its graph never goes below the x-axis in the interval $[a, b]$). Then the area bounded by the graph of $f(x)$, the x-axis, and the lines $x = a$ and $x = b$, may be evaluated as follows:

The area described is that shown in Figure 4.1(a).

(a) Find an integral $F(x)$ of $f(x)$.
(b) Calculate the difference in the values of the function F between a and b, that is, $F(b) - F(a)$.

We emphasise that so far this is just a hypothesis, which is based only on the two simple cases looked at in Activities 4.1 and 4.2. However, it turns out to be correct, and we shall provide more justification for this claim shortly.

Before doing so, we introduce some new notation and make an important definition. The difference in the values of a function at two points in its domain, as in $F(b) - F(a)$ above, occurs sufficiently frequently in calculus to have been abbreviated. We write

$$F(b) - F(a) = [F(x)]_a^b,$$

which is sometimes shortened further to $[F]_a^b$. This is pronounced as 'F(x) (or F) evaluated from a to b'.

Activity 4.3   Evaluating functions from a to b

Evaluate each of the following.

(a) $\left[\frac{1}{2}x^2\right]_3^5$ (b) $[\cos x]_0^{2\pi}$ (c) $[\exp x]_{-1}^1$

Comment

Solutions are given on page 75.

The hypothesis stated above, for the evaluation of areas, depends on two steps which are not in themselves obviously related to area. These are as follows, given a continuous function $f(x)$ and two values a and b in its domain:

(a) Find an integral $F(x)$ of $f(x)$.
(b) Calculate the difference $[F(x)]_a^b = F(b) - F(a)$.

The outcome of these two steps is known as the *definite integral* of the function $f(x)$ from a to b. The value of such a definite integral is the same whichever integral of $f(x)$ is chosen. This is so because if $F(x)$ is one such integral, then any other is equal to $F(x) + c$ for some constant c, and we have

$$[F(x) + c]_a^b = F(b) + c - F(a) - c = [F(x)]_a^b.$$

Thus the outcome can also be written in terms of the *indefinite* integral

$$\int f(x)\, dx = F(x) + c,$$

where c is an arbitrary constant. In fact, the definite integral is equal to

$$\left[\int f(x)\,dx\right]_a^b,$$

and this in turn is abbreviated to

$$\int_a^b f(x)\,dx.$$

In this expression for the definite integral, the numbers a and b are called the *limits of integration* with a being the *lower limit* and b the *upper limit*.

Definition

The **definite integral** of a continuous function $f(x)$ from a to b, denoted by

$$\int_a^b f(x)\,dx,$$

is defined to be

$$[F(x)]_a^b = F(b) - F(a),$$

where $F(x)$ is any integral of $f(x)$.

Symbols other than x can be used for the variable of integration *without altering the outcome*, since that outcome is simply a number. Thus we have

$$\int_a^b f(x)\,dx = \int_a^b f(t)\,dt = \int_a^b f(u)\,du = \dots,$$

since all of these expressions equal $F(b) - F(a)$. For this reason, the variable of integration is sometimes called a *dummy variable*.

The definite integral may also be written without an explicit variable of integration, as

$$\int_a^b f.$$

Example 4.1   Evaluating a definite integral

Evaluate the definite integral

$$\int_0^\pi \sin x \, dx.$$

Solution

An integral of $\sin x$ is $-\cos x$. Hence we have

$$\int_0^\pi \sin x \, dx = [-\cos x]_0^\pi$$
$$= -\cos \pi - (-\cos 0)$$
$$= -(-1) - (-1) = 2.$$

Activity 4.4   Definite integrals

Evaluate each of the following definite integrals.

(a) $\displaystyle\int_{-1}^1 x^2\,dx$ (b) $\displaystyle\int_0^2 \exp t \, dt$ (c) $\displaystyle\int_1^4 \frac{1}{u}\,du$

Comment

Solutions are given on page 75.

In terms of the definition given above for the definite integral, our earlier hypothesis about areas under graphs can be restated as follows.

Finding the area under a graph

If $f(x)$ is a continuous function which takes no negative values for $a \leq x \leq b$, then the area bounded by the graph of $f(x)$, the x-axis, and the lines $x = a$ and $x = b$, is equal to the definite integral

$$\int_a^b f(x)\,dx.$$

We claimed earlier that this statement is correct, and we now give an explanation of why this is so.

Suppose that $f(x)$ is a continuous function which takes non-negative values only on the interval $[a, b]$. Then, for each value of x in the interval, let $A(x)$ denote the area under the graph of $f(x)$ from a to x, as shown in Figure 4.4 below. This may be called the *area-so-far function*, where the 'so far' is measured from the starting value a. Thus we have $A(a) = 0$, while $A(b)$ denotes the area under the graph of $f(x)$ from a to b.

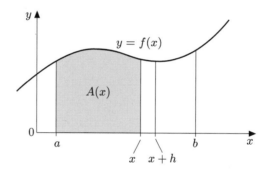

Figure 4.4

On this diagram we have also drawn the vertical line through $x + h$, where h is a small positive amount. Now consider the region under the graph of $f(x)$ from x to $x + h$. On the one hand, the area of this region must equal

$$A(x + h) - A(x),$$

from the definition of the area-so-far function. On the other hand, this region is a strip of width h, and its area is close to that of a rectangle of width h and height $f(x)$, so we can write

$$A(x + h) - A(x) \simeq hf(x).$$

The percentage error involved in approximating the narrow region by a rectangle decreases to the limit zero as h is reduced towards zero, so on dividing through by h and then taking the limit as $h \to 0$, we find that

$$\lim_{h \to 0} \left[\frac{A(x + h) - A(x)}{h} \right] = f(x).$$

The expression on the left-hand side, as you may remember from the definition in Chapter C1, is the *derivative* of $A(x)$, so we have

Chapter C1 Subsection 2.2

$$A'(x) = f(x).$$

We also have an initial condition for $A(x)$ since, as noted above,

$A(a) = 0.$

Thus the area-so-far function $A(x)$ satisfies the initial-value problem

$A'(x) = f(x), \quad A(a) = 0.$

To find the solution of this problem, suppose that $F(x)$ is *any* integral of $f(x)$. Then $A(x)$, which is another such integral, must be equal to $F(x) + c$ for some constant c. Using the initial condition, we have

$A(a) = F(a) + c = 0,$

so that $c = -F(a)$. We conclude that, if $F(x)$ is any integral of $f(x)$, then the area-so-far function can be expressed in terms of the function F as

$A(x) = F(x) - F(a).$

In particular, on putting $x = b$, we obtain

$A(b) = F(b) - F(a)$

$= \int_a^b f(x)\,dx.$

This concludes the argument that the hypothesis stated above is valid. We now put this result to use.

Example 4.2   Finding an area by definite integration

Find the area under the graph of $\sin x$ from $x = 0$ to $x = \pi$ (see Figure 4.5).

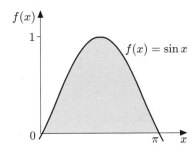

Figure 4.5

Solution

The area is equal to the definite integral

$\int_0^\pi \sin x\,dx,$

whose value was found in Example 4.1 to be 2.

(As a check, note that this region is enclosed within a rectangle of base π and height 1, which has area $\pi > 2$, and encloses a triangle of base π and height 1, which has area $\frac{1}{2}\pi < 2$.)

Activity 4.5   Finding areas by definite integration

(a) Find the area under the graph of x^2 from $x = -1$ to $x = 1$ (see Figure 4.6(a)).

(b) Find the area under the graph of $\exp(-3t)$ from $t = 0$ to $t = \frac{2}{3}$ (see Figure 4.6(b)).

(c) Using the fact that $u(\ln u - 1)$ is an integral of $\ln u$, find the area under the graph of $\ln u$ from $u = 1$ to $u = 2$ (see Figure 4.6(c)).

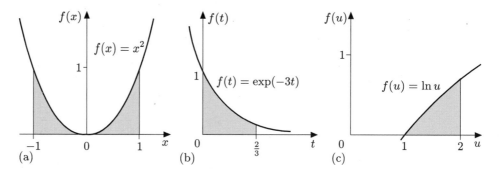

Figure 4.6

Comment

Solutions are given on page 75.

To conclude this subsection, note that definite integrals do not always represent areas. As was said above, if $f(x)$ is a continuous function on the interval $[a, b]$, and if $f(x) \geq 0$ for all x in this interval, then the definite integral

$$\int_a^b f(x)\, dx$$

does give the value of the area under the graph of $f(x)$ from a to b. However, if we have $f(x) < 0$ for some x in $[a, b]$, then the definite integral above will not represent an area.

For example, you saw in Example 4.2 that the area under the graph of $\sin x$ from $x = 0$ to $x = \pi$ is

$$\int_0^\pi \sin x\, dx = 2.$$

On the other hand, we also have

$$\int_\pi^{2\pi} \sin x\, dx = [-\cos x]_\pi^{2\pi}$$
$$= -\cos(2\pi) - (-\cos \pi)$$
$$= -1 - (-(-1)) = -2.$$

This cannot be the value of an area, since it is negative. A look at the graph of $\sin x$ shows what has happened (see Figure 4.7). This graph is below the x-axis in the interval $[\pi, 2\pi]$, so that $\sin x < 0$ in this interval.

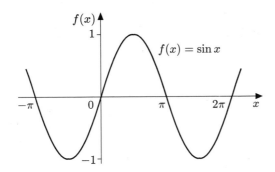

Figure 4.7

Even when the definite integral is positive, it may not correspond to an area. Thus we obtain

$$\int_0^{3\pi/2} \sin x\, dx = [-\cos x]_0^{3\pi/2}$$
$$= -\cos(\tfrac{3}{2}\pi) - (-\cos 0)$$
$$= 0 - (-1) = 1$$

but, as Figure 4.7 shows, $\sin x$ takes negative as well as positive values on the interval $[0, 3\pi/2]$.

Activity 4.6   Which are areas?

Which of the following definite integrals

$$\int_a^b f(x)\, dx$$

represent the area under the graph of $f(x)$ from a to b?

(a) $\displaystyle\int_{-1}^1 x\, dx$ (b) $\displaystyle\int_{-1}^1 x^2\, dx$ (c) $\displaystyle\int_0^{3\pi/4} \cos x\, dx$

Comment

Solutions are given on page 75.

Finding areas is just one of the many applications of the definite integral. Another is the calculation of change of position, given a velocity function. If an object moving along a straight line has velocity $v(t)$ at time t, for $a \le t \le b$, then the total change of position of the object between times a and b is given by

$$\int_a^b v(t)\, dt.$$

In this case the representation is valid without restriction on the sign of $v(t)$.

4.2 The definite integral as a limit of summations

The definite integral method for finding areas under a graph, described in the last subsection, has a potential drawback. It depends on being able to identify an integral $F(x)$ of the original function $f(x)$ under whose graph the area is to be found, but sometimes there is no simple formula which can be found for such an integral. The area must then be sought by alternative means.

In this subsection we investigate an alternative approach to finding the area beneath a graph. This turns out to have an extra pay-off, in that it leads to an illuminating second view of what the definite integral is, and some modelling applications of this second view are presented in Section 5.

Designing a sports hall

Imagine that you are an architect who has been commissioned to design a large sports hall. The brief which you were given has led you to specify a rectangular base for the hall, of length 80 m and width 40 m, with a roof which has a uniform cross-section across the width and a central height of 15 m. You decide that this cross-section of the roof should have a pleasing sweep like that shown in Figure 4.8. You choose the function

$$f(x) = 15\sqrt{\sin\left(\frac{\pi x}{40}\right)}$$

to describe the height of this cross-section, since this gives a nearly vertical wall close to the two sides.

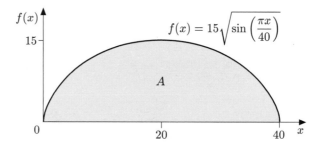

Figure 4.8

One of the pieces of information which you are asked to provide is the overall volume of the hall, so that the power supply required to heat the air inside can be determined. This volume is $80A\,\mathrm{m}^3$, where $A\,\mathrm{m}^2$ is the cross-sectional area shown above.

You therefore need to calculate this area. It can be expressed in terms of a definite integral as

$$A = \int_0^{40} 15\sqrt{\sin\left(\frac{\pi x}{40}\right)}\,dx,$$

but there is no simple formula known for an integral of the function

$$f(x) = 15\sqrt{\sin\left(\frac{\pi x}{40}\right)}.$$

You are therefore forced to consider an alternative approach. Your first thought might be to obtain very rough upper and lower bounds on the area A of the shaded region. It is enclosed within a rectangle of base 40 and height 15, so that $A < 600$. It encloses a triangle of the same base and height, so that $A > 300$.

One approach to obtaining a closer estimate for A is to approximate the region under the graph by a collection of rectangles, with the estimate being the sum of their areas. A step in this direction is illustrated in Figure 4.9.

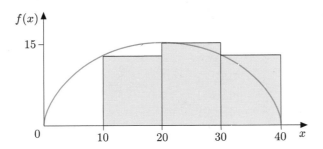

Figure 4.9

The interval $[0, 40]$ has been divided into four equal subintervals, and on each a rectangle has been constructed so that its top left corner meets the graph of $f(x)$ (the leftmost 'rectangle' therefore has height zero). The area A is approximated by the sum of the areas of these rectangles, which is

$$10 \times f(0) + 10 \times f(10) + 10 \times f(20) + 10 \times f(30)$$

$$= 10 \left(0 + 15 \sqrt{\sin \left(\frac{10\pi}{40} \right)} + 15 \sqrt{\sin \left(\frac{20\pi}{40} \right)} + 15 \sqrt{\sin \left(\frac{30\pi}{40} \right)} \right)$$

$$= 150 \left(\sqrt{\sin \left(\frac{\pi}{4} \right)} + \sqrt{\sin \left(\frac{\pi}{2} \right)} + \sqrt{\sin \left(\frac{3\pi}{4} \right)} \right)$$

$$= 150(0.840896 + 1 + 0.840896) = 402.27.$$

An improvement to this estimate for A can be found by dividing up the interval $[0, 40]$ into a larger number of subintervals, since the rectangles will then overlap more closely the region beneath the graph. With 20 subintervals of width 2, for example, the same construction produces the collection of rectangles shown in Figure 4.10.

Note that this and the further estimates below all lie within the range $300 < A < 600$ which was established with the rough lower and upper bounds.

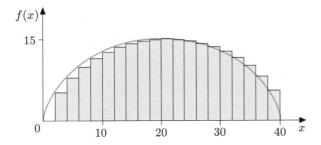

Figure 4.10

The sum of the areas of these rectangles is

$$2 \times f(0) + 2 \times f(2) + 2 \times f(4) + \cdots + 2 \times f(38)$$

$$= 2 \times 15 \left(\sqrt{\sin \left(\frac{2\pi}{40} \right)} + \sqrt{\sin \left(\frac{4\pi}{40} \right)} + \cdots + \sqrt{\sin \left(\frac{38\pi}{40} \right)} \right)$$

$$= 452.71.$$

You are *not* expected to check by hand this and the similar calculations below. The answers were obtained using the Mathcad summation facility, and you will be able to use this to check some of the results in Subsection 4.3.

53

This is the estimate for A based upon 20 subintervals. Further improvements can be found by increasing successively the number of subintervals into which the interval $[0, 40]$ is divided. Table 4.1 below shows results obtained in this way.

Table 4.1

Number of subintervals	Sum of areas of rectangles
4	402.27
20	452.71
50	456.41
100	457.21
500	457.62
1 000	457.64
5 000	457.66
10 000	457.66

The convergence of the values in the right-hand column suggests that we have

$$A = \int_0^{40} 15\sqrt{\sin\left(\frac{\pi x}{40}\right)}\, dx = 457.66$$

to two decimal places. Thus the volume of the hall is

$$80A = 36\,613\,\mathrm{m}^3.$$

It would probably suffice to quote this to the nearest $100\,\mathrm{m}^3$, as $36\,600\,\mathrm{m}^3$.

Generalising the approach

The calculation of the area A above was achieved without recourse to finding an integral of the given function $f(x)$ whose graph bounded the region of interest. It is possible to generalise this result, and hence to formulate a method of definite integration which relies upon computer power rather than on finding a formula for the integral of a function.

Suppose that $f(x)$ is any function which is continuous and non-negative on the interval $[a, b]$. We shall seek the area under the graph of $f(x)$ from a to b, which is the area of the shaded region in Figure 4.11 below, and is equal to the definite integral

$$\int_a^b f(x)\, dx.$$

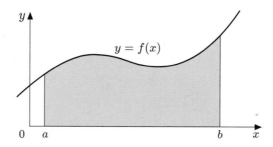

Figure 4.11

The interval $[a, b]$ is divided into N equal subintervals of width

$$h = \frac{b - a}{N},$$

where N is any positive integer. These N subintervals are

$$[a, a + h], [a + h, a + 2h], [a + 2h, a + 3h], \ldots,$$

with the Nth and final interval being

$$[a + (N - 1)h, a + Nh] = [b - h, b].$$

This can also be expressed by saying that the $(i + 1)$th subinterval is

$$[a + ih, a + (i + 1)h] \quad (i = 0, 1, 2, \ldots, N - 1).$$

On each subinterval, we construct a rectangle whose top left corner lies on the graph of $f(x)$, as indicated in Figure 4.12.

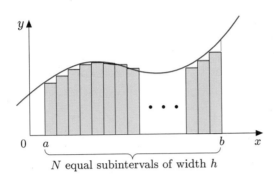

Figure 4.12

For the $(i + 1)$th subinterval, the height of the corresponding rectangle is then $f(a + ih)$, and its area is

$$hf(a + ih) \quad (i = 0, 1, 2, \ldots, N - 1).$$

The sum of the areas of the N rectangles so constructed is

$$\sum_{i=0}^{N-1} hf(a + ih), \quad \text{where } h = \frac{b - a}{N}. \tag{4.1}$$

For each positive integer N, the sum (4.1) gives an approximate estimate of the area

$$\int_a^b f(x)\, dx.$$

Arguing as in the specific case of the sports hall roof considered earlier, the approximation (4.1) becomes closer and closer to the actual value of the area as N increases. Another way of expressing this convergence in the values of the sums is to say that the definite integral is equal to the *limit* of these values for ever larger N, which is written as

$$\int_a^b f(x)\, dx = \lim_{N \to \infty} \left[\sum_{i=0}^{N-1} hf(a + ih) \right], \quad \text{where } h = \frac{b - a}{N}. \tag{4.2}$$

This is a more complicated limit than that which appeared in the definition of the derivative, since as $N \to \infty$ we have also $h \to 0$, while the product Nh remains fixed at the value $b - a$. As N increases, the sum in the square brackets consists of more and more terms, but each individual term makes a smaller and smaller contribution to the whole.

Chapter C1 Subsection 2.2

We have deduced equation (4.2) with reference to finding the area under a curve, for which the associated function $f(x)$ was taken to be non-negative in the interval $[a, b]$. However, it turns out that equation (4.2) applies to *any* continuous function $f(x)$, without restriction on the sign of the values which $f(x)$ takes. This result therefore provides a means of finding the numerical value of any definite integral.

While we have argued that equation (4.2) is a plausible result, we have not proved its validity, and such a proof is beyond the scope of this course. However, the result is of great importance and usefulness. It carries the name of the *Fundamental Theorem of Calculus*. Indeed, many texts take equation (4.2) as the *definition* of the definite integral. This brings the concept of integration into line with its everyday meaning of 'combining parts into a whole'.

Fundamental Theorem of Calculus

If $f(x)$ is a function which is continuous on the interval $[a, b]$, then

$$\int_a^b f(x)\,dx = \lim_{N \to \infty} \left[\sum_{i=0}^{N-1} h f(a + ih) \right], \quad \text{where } h = \frac{b-a}{N}. \quad (4.2)$$

It is possible at this point to provide some explanation of where the

$$\int \ldots dx$$

notation for integrals comes from. Suppose that we replace the subinterval length h by δx ('a small increase in x'), as we did in explaining the Leibniz notation for derivatives at the end of Chapter C1, Subsection 2.3. If we also write

$$x_i = a + ih \quad (i = 0, 1, 2, \ldots, N - 1),$$

then equation (4.2) becomes

As mentioned in Chapter C1, you may also see Δx rather than δx in such expressions.

$$\int_a^b f(x)\,dx = \lim_{\delta x \to 0} \left[\sum_{i=0}^{N-1} f(x_i)\delta x \right], \quad \text{where } N\delta x = b - a.$$

The elongated S of the integral sign denotes a 'limiting sum', and the dx at the end of the integral is a 'residue' of the δx which appears in each sum on the right-hand side.

Other versions of the summation process described in deriving equation (4.2) lead to a similar outcome. We chose to construct the rectangle on each subinterval so that its height was equal to the function value at the left-hand end of the subinterval. It suffices in fact for the height of this rectangle to equal the function value at *any* point within the subinterval concerned. For example, this point could be taken at the right-hand end of each subinterval, or at its centre. The limit of the sums so created still gives the value of the definite integral.

There have been no activities for you to carry out in this subsection. This is because the results introduced here require the use of a computer for their implementation in practical cases, and you are invited to investigate how this can be achieved using Mathcad in the next subsection.

Mathcad cannot in fact 'take a limit' to evaluate the right-hand side of equation (4.2) in specific cases. However, in practice all that is required is that the sum (4.1) should give the same value, to a specified accuracy, for two large but widely separated values of N (say for one value twice as large as the other). You saw this strategy demonstrated in Table 4.1 on page 54 and in the conclusion drawn from it.

4.3 Definite integrals in Mathcad

In Section 2 you put the Mathcad 'indefinite integral' operator to use, which produces *an* integral of a function rather than what we defined earlier as the indefinite integral (featuring an arbitrary constant). Mathcad also has facilities to deal with definite integrals, and they are the focus of this subsection.

In Subsection 4.1, you saw that if $f(x)$ is a continuous function, then the definite integral

$$\int_a^b f(x)\,dx$$

can be evaluated by finding an integral $F(x)$ of $f(x)$, and then calculating the difference

$$[F(x)]_a^b = F(b) - F(a).$$

In fact, this was how we defined the definite integral.

In Subsection 4.2, you saw an alternative approach based on the 'limiting sum' formula for the definite integral,

$$\int_a^b f(x)\,dx = \lim_{N\to\infty} \left[\sum_{i=0}^{N-1} h f(a + ih) \right], \quad \text{where } h = \frac{b-a}{N}. \qquad (4.2)$$

As you will see, Mathcad can operate with either the symbolic approach from Subsection 4.1 or a numerical approach akin to that of Subsection 4.2. Its version of the symbolic strategy is limited to those functions for which it can find an integral. Its alternative numerical strategy is more sophisticated than the one we described in Subsection 4.2, but is similar in principle.

Refer to Computer Book C for the work in this subsection.

Earlier, we specified the range of functions for which you would be expected to find indefinite integrals 'by hand'. These were the functions given in Table 1.1 on page 20, augmented by use of the Constant Multiple and Sum Rules for integrals.

As far as definite integrals are concerned, the same applies. You are expected to be able to find the definite integral of any continuous function in the range just described, over any interval in the domain of such a function. Other cases may be dealt with, either symbolically or numerically, using the Mathcad definite integral facilities.

Summary of Section 4

In this section, definite integrals were introduced.

◇   The *definite integral* of a continuous function $f(x)$ from a to b, denoted by

$$\int_a^b f(x)\,dx,$$

is defined to be

$$[F(x)]_a^b = F(b) - F(a),$$

where $F(x)$ is any integral of $f(x)$.

◇   If $f(x)$ is a continuous function which takes no negative values for $a \leq x \leq b$, then the area bounded by the graph of $f(x)$, the x-axis, and the lines $x = a$ and $x = b$, is equal to the definite integral

$$\int_a^b f(x)\, dx.$$

◇   The *Fundamental Theorem of Calculus* states that if $f(x)$ is a function which is continuous on the interval $[a, b]$, then

$$\int_a^b f(x)\, dx = \lim_{N \to \infty} \left[\sum_{i=0}^{N-1} h f(a + ih) \right], \quad \text{where } h = \frac{b - a}{N}.$$

◇   You are expected in MST121 to be able to find definite integrals 'by hand' in any case for which the function to be integrated appears in Table 1.1 on page 20, or is related to such functions by the Constant Multiple and Sum Rules for integrals. Alternatively, an integral for the function may be given.

Exercises for Section 4

Exercise 4.1

Evaluate each of the following definite integrals.

(a) $\displaystyle\int_0^{\pi/4} (\cos(5x) + 2\sin(5x))\, dx$

(b) $\displaystyle\int_1^2 \frac{6}{u^2}\, du$

(c) $\displaystyle\int_0^{\pi} e^t \sin t\, dt$,   given that $\frac{1}{2} e^t (\sin t - \cos t)$ is an integral of $e^t \sin t$.

Exercise 4.2

(a) Find the area under the graph of $2x^3$ from $x = 1$ to $x = 2$.

(b) Find the area above the x-axis which is also bounded by the graph of $x(3 - x)$.

(c) Using the fact that $\arctan x$ is an integral of $(1 + x^2)^{-1}$, find the area under the graph of $(1 + x^2)^{-1}$ from $x = -2$ to $x = 2$.

5 Further applications of definite integrals

In this section you will see how definite integrals can arise in the course of constructing a mathematical model, by starting with a discrete approximation and then taking an appropriate limit. The transition from the discrete to the continuous depends upon an appeal to equation (4.2), which represents the definite integral as a limit of discrete summations.

The first subsection concerns a simple model of the population distribution in a town, and the second looks at water flowing along a pipe. The technique of setting up an integral which is demonstrated in these two examples has many further applications.

5.1 Population in a town

Suppose that a town has grown up around a central road, and that its extent is modelled by a rectangle of width 6 km and length 10 km, with the road represented by a straight line AB down the middle of its length (see Figure 5.1).

The model described here is greatly simplified. However, it suffices to demonstrate a modelling approach which also applies in more realistic cases.

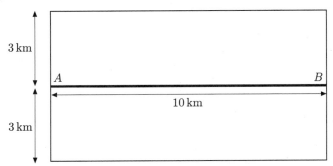

Figure 5.1

A recent census indicates that the town has a total population of 35 000 people. The census also suggests that the distribution of the population depends only on distance from the road. In fact, a simple model for the population density $p(y)$ (number of people per km^2) at position y in the direction perpendicular to the road is

$$p(y) = p_0 \cos\left(\frac{\pi y}{6}\right) \quad (-3 \le y \le 3), \tag{5.1}$$

where p_0 is a constant. On putting $y = 0$ in this equation, it can be seen that $p_0 = p(0)$, which is the value of the population density at the road AB. The value of p_0 is not yet known, but will be determined by the size of the total population.

Imagine that the road AB is heavily congested, because it carries a large amount of through traffic, and that in consequence there is significant noise and air pollution close to the road. A pressure group has been set up to encourage town planners to build a bypass which will relieve the road AB of the through traffic. A recent survey suggests that the people living within one kilometre of the road are strongly affected by the noise and air pollution.

As a member of the pressure group, you are asked to estimate the number of people who are strongly affected by the pollution from the through traffic. The pressure group can use this information in persuading the town planners to build a new bypass.

Activity 5.1   What to find?

(a) On the basis of the text above, what precisely are you being asked to find and what information do you have initially at your disposal?

(b) What do you think 'population density' means? Note that the function given for population density in equation (5.1) varies continuously as y increases.

Comment

(a) You want to find the number of people living within the reduced region $-1 \le y \le 1$, which is shown shaded in Figure 5.2 below.

Figure 5.2

You know that:

(i) the extent of the town is modelled by the larger rectangle shown in Figure 5.2, that is, the region $-3 \le y \le 3$;

(ii) the total population of the town is 35 000;

(iii) the population density $p(y)$ people per km² is given by

$$p(y) = p_0 \cos\left(\frac{\pi y}{6}\right) \quad (-3 \le y \le 3), \tag{5.1}$$

where the constant p_0 is unknown.

(b) If P people live in a region of area A km², then the *average* population density of the region is $p = P/A$ people per km². Given a population density p people per km² which is *constant* over a region of area A km², the population of the region is $P = pA$ people.

Given a population density $p(x, y)$ which *varies* over a region of the (x, y)-plane, the situation is more complicated. We can say that, if A km² is the area of a *small* subregion surrounding any point (x, y) in the region, then the population of this small subregion is approximately $p(x, y)A$. The approximation arises because we are taking the value of p at one point within the subregion to represent the values of p at all points in the subregion.

This approximation to the population of the subregion will tend to have a smaller percentage error if the area of the subregion is reduced, since the variation of $p(x, y)$ within the subregion will then be less. In the current situation, we have $p(y)$ rather than $p(x, y)$, since the population density varies in the y-direction only.

Actually there is more to it than this, since a *very* small subregion either has a person (or part of one) within it or it doesn't! A continuous population density in effect treats people as if 'continuously distributed' over the region of interest.

Before reaching the eventual aim identified in Activity 5.1(a), you need to find the value of the constant p_0, which requires a link to be made between the population density

$$p(y) = p_0 \cos\left(\frac{\pi y}{6}\right) \quad (-3 \le y \le 3) \tag{5.1}$$

and the total population 35 000 of the town. It is possible to construct an expression for the total population which depends upon the population density at each point. However, it is sufficient to consider just half of the town, for $0 \le y \le 3$ say, since the population density function (5.1) is symmetric about $y = 0$, that is, $p(y) = p(-y)$.

Following the comment for Activity 5.1(b), we need to identify convenient regions over which the value of the population density does not vary much. This can be done by dividing the upper half of the rectangle which represents the town into N narrow strips parallel to AB, each of length 10 km and width h km, as shown in Figure 5.3 below. For these strips to cover half the town, we must have $Nh = 3$.

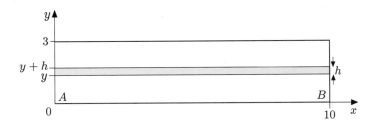

Figure 5.3

The area of each strip is $10h$ km^2. If h is sufficiently small, then $p(y)$ will not vary much over each strip, and we may take its value at any point within the strip to obtain a population estimate for the strip as a whole.

The first strip extends from $y = 0$ to $y = h$, the second from $y = h$ to $y = 2h$, and so on. The $(i+1)$th strip extends from $y = ih$ to $y = (i+1)h$ $(i = 0, 1, 2, \ldots, N-1)$. Hence a population estimate for the $(i+1)$th strip is

$p(ih) \times 10h$ people,

which leads to an estimate for all the strips together of

$$\sum_{i=0}^{N-1} 10p(ih)h, \quad \text{where } Nh = 3. \tag{5.2}$$

This sum can also be written as

$$\sum_{i=0}^{N-1} 10p(y_i)\delta y,$$

where $y_i = ih$ and $\delta y = h$.

Perhaps you can now see where this is leading. For any number N of strips, we have an estimate for the population of half the town, and this estimate becomes better and better as N increases, since each strip of width h then becomes narrower and narrower. The 'best estimate' is therefore obtained by taking the limit of expression (5.2) as $N \to \infty$. According to equation (4.2), the result of doing this is the definite integral

$$10 \int_0^3 p(y)\,dy = \lim_{N\to\infty}\left[\sum_{i=0}^{N-1} 10p(ih)h\right], \quad \text{where } Nh = 3. \tag{5.3}$$

To compare with equation (4.2), put $10p$ in place of f, y in place of x, $a = 0$ and $b = 3$.

We now use equation (5.1) to insert the specific function given for p, and double the result so as to account for both halves of the town. This gives

$$20p_0 \int_0^3 \cos\left(\frac{\pi y}{6}\right) dy = 35\,000,$$

or

$$p_0 \int_0^3 \cos\left(\frac{\pi y}{6}\right) dy = 1750.$$

Activity 5.2   Evaluating the integral

By evaluating the definite integral

$$\int_0^3 \cos\left(\frac{\pi y}{6}\right) dy,$$

find the value of p_0.

Comment

A solution is given on page 76.

Your answer to Activity 5.2 shows that the population of the town is given approximately by

$$p(y) = 916 \cos\left(\frac{\pi y}{6}\right) \quad (-3 \le y \le 3).$$

Activity 5.3   Completing the task

Complete your task for the pressure group, by estimating how many people live within one kilometre of the road. (There is no need to set up an integral from scratch here. Just identify what has to change in the argument above for the whole town.)

Comment

A solution is given on page 76.

According to your answer to Activity 5.3, the model provides an estimate of 17 500 people living within one kilometre of the road. The pressure group could therefore put forward a reasonable case that half of the population of the town are adversely affected by the noise and air pollution due to through traffic on the central road.

The procedure which was employed above can be summarised as follows.

Procedure for setting up an integral

◇ Identify the independent variable of interest (the position relative to the road AB in this case, denoted by y).

◇ Set up a discrete model by dividing the area into narrow strips, whose long boundaries correspond to constant values for this independent variable.

◇ Find an estimate for the required quantity in each strip (here the 'required quantity' was the population).

◇ Add up the required quantities for each strip to obtain a summation.

◇ Increase the number of strips indefinitely (and correspondingly let the width of each strip tend to zero) to obtain a continuous model based on a definite integral.

The advantage of having a model which features a definite integral is that calculus techniques can then be employed to evaluate this integral.

Activity 5.4   Same town, different time

Suppose that, thirty years ago, the town occupied the same region of land. Its total population was 20 000, and its population density could be modelled by the function

$$p(y) = \begin{cases} p_0 \exp(y) & (-3 \le y < 0), \\ p_0 \exp(-y) & (0 \le y \le 3). \end{cases}$$

Estimate how many people then lived within one kilometre of the central road.

Comment

A solution is given on page 76.

5.2 Flow in a circular pipe

The procedure for setting up integrals, as described above, is very useful in the modelling of problems in one dimension or where, as in the case of the town's population density, the function being considered varies only with changes to one of the possible independent variables and is constant with respect to changes in any others.

When the region which forms the domain of an important function in the model is rectangular, then it is natural to choose the independent variables as standard Cartesian coordinates, with x- and y-axes parallel to the sides of the rectangle. On the other hand, when the region concerned is circular, then it is often more appropriate to choose the origin to be at the centre of the circle, with the radial coordinate r as one of the independent variables. With this change, the method of 'taking narrow strips' may still be applied in appropriate cases, and you will see here examples which demonstrate this.

Area of a circle

The simplest such example concerns just finding the area of a circle. You probably know that the area of a circle of radius R is πR^2, but where does this formula come from?

Note first that the number π is defined as the ratio of the circumference to the diameter of any circle. Hence, for a circle of radius r, the circumference is $2\pi r$.

We now apply the procedure for setting up integrals, as given on page 62, but on this occasion the 'narrow strips' will be bounded by circles rather than by straight lines.

Each of these strips has the shape of an *annulus*.

Choose the origin at the centre of the circle of radius R, whose area is sought, and let r denote radial distance from the origin. This area can be divided into N narrow strips of width h, as shown in Figure 5.4 below, where $Nh = R$.

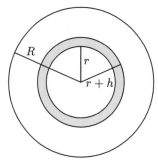

Figure 5.4

The $(i+1)$th strip extends from $r = ih$ to $r = (i+1)h$ $(i = 0, 1, 2, \ldots, N-1)$. The circumference of its inner boundary is $2\pi r = 2\pi ih$, and its width is h, so its area is approximately $(2\pi ih)h$. Adding up the approximate areas of all N strips, we obtain an estimate for the area of the whole circle as

$$\sum_{i=0}^{N-1} (2\pi ih)h, \quad \text{where } Nh = R.$$

This sum can also be written as

$$\sum_{i=0}^{N-1} (2\pi r_i)\delta r,$$

where $r_i = ih$ and $\delta r = h$. The approximation becomes exact in the limit as $N \to \infty$, to give

$$\int_0^R 2\pi r\, dr = \lim_{N \to \infty} \left[\sum_{i=0}^{N-1} (2\pi ih)h \right], \quad \text{where } Nh = R.$$

Activity 5.5   Area of a circle

Complete the calculation, in order to derive the formula for the area of a circle of radius R.

Comment

A solution is given on page 76.

The approach demonstrated above applies equally well to other situations relating to circular regions, where there is a radial symmetry involved.

Flow in a pipe

When a liquid flows along a pipe, it is of interest to know how the volume rate at which it moves is related to its velocity and to the internal dimensions of the pipe. This relationship has application to the study of blood flow along arteries, and also in the modelling of any system of water supply.

In what follows, we concentrate on the case of water flowing along a rigid pipe whose cross-section is uniform and circular. The flow is also assumed to be uniform, in the sense that the velocity profile of the water will be the same over any cross-section perpendicular to the axis of the pipe.

If water flows through a pipe perpendicular to an area $A\,\mathrm{m}^2$ with a velocity $v_0\,\mathrm{m\,s}^{-1}$ that does not vary across the area, then the corresponding volume flow rate is $v_0 A\,\mathrm{m}^3\mathrm{s}^{-1}$ (cubic metres per second). This is illustrated in Figure 5.5 below, which can be thought of as showing the volume of water which flows across the area in one second.

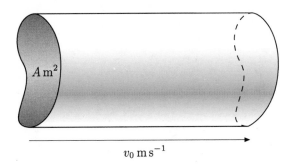

$$v_0\,\mathrm{m\,s}^{-1}$$

Figure 5.5

Activity 5.6   A simple model

If the velocity $v_0\,\mathrm{m\,s}^{-1}$ of the water flowing along a circular pipe of radius $R\,\mathrm{m}$ is constant across a cross-section of the pipe, what is the volume flow rate through the pipe?

Comment

A solution is given on page 76.

The simple model which you considered in Activity 5.6 gives results which are far from those observed experimentally. One important factor which this model does not take into account is the effect of liquid friction or *viscosity*. This slows the water down progressively as the wall of the pipe is approached, although the velocity at any particular radial distance from the centre may still be approximately constant. A model of viscous flow, that is, flow with viscosity, predicts that the velocity profile within a cross-section for a circular pipe of radius R is given by

$$v(r) = v_0\left(1 - \left(\frac{r}{R}\right)^2\right), \tag{5.4}$$

where v_0 is a constant. This prediction agrees with experimental results in a range of cases.

Activity 5.7   Flow velocity function

Suppose that the flow velocity of the water in the pipe is as described by equation (5.4).

(a) What does the constant v_0 represent?

(b) What is the velocity at the wall of the pipe?

(c) Sketch the graph of the flow velocity $v(r)$ as a function of the distance r from the centre of the pipe.

Comment

Solutions are given on page 76.

In calculating the area of a circle, we divided the region up into a number of narrow annular strips, and we can proceed in a similar way here. To assist with visualising what is going on, think of the flow as being in layers which slide over one another, with each layer having the form of a thin cylindrical shell (see Figure 5.6 below). The velocity increases as the layers approach the centre of the pipe, and decreases towards zero at the pipe wall.

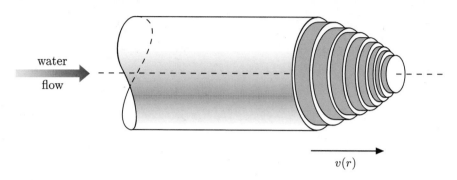

Figure 5.6

Each layer is sufficiently narrow for the velocity change across it to be ignored in a first approximation. If length represents velocity, as in Figure 5.6, then the corresponding volume of a layer represents the volume rate of flow. The cross-section of each layer perpendicular to the flow is one of the annular strips.

Suppose that there are N such strips, each of width h, with the $(i+1)$th strip extending from $r = ih$ to $r = (i+1)h$ $(i = 0, 1, 2, \ldots, N-1)$. In the extended Activity below, you are asked to continue with this argument, to obtain a definite integral for the volume flow rate along the pipe.

Activity 5.8   Finding the volume flow rate

(a) What is the value of Nh?

(b) What is the approximate area of the $(i+1)$th annular strip?

(c) What is the velocity $v(r)$ of the water at the inside boundary of the $(i+1)$th strip?

(d) Write down an expression for the approximate volume flow rate of water across the $(i+1)$th strip.

(e) Write down an expression for the approximate volume flow rate of water across the entire cross-section of the pipe.

(f) Take the limit of your expression in part (e) as $N \to \infty$, and apply equation (4.2) to obtain a definite integral.

(g) By evaluating this definite integral for the case

$$v(r) = v_0 \left(1 - \left(\frac{r}{R} \right)^2 \right), \tag{5.4}$$

find the volume flow rate along the pipe in terms of v_0 and R.

Comment

Solutions are given on page 77.

In Activity 5.6 you showed that the simple model for flow in a pipe, in which the velocity $v(r) = v_0$ is the same for all values of r, gives the prediction $\pi v_0 R^2$ for the volume flow rate. In Activity 5.8 you showed that, in a model which takes viscosity into account and where v_0 represents velocity along the pipe axis, the volume flow rate is predicted to be $\frac{1}{2}\pi v_0 R^2$. This second prediction turns out to be a good one when compared with many experiments.

The approach to setting up definite integrals within a model, as introduced in this section, has many further applications. As was pointed out earlier, it depends essentially on the Fundamental Theorem of Calculus, as embodied in equation (4.2).

Summary of Section 5

In this section you have seen an approach to setting up integrals which is useful for modelling purposes.

◇   The procedure for setting up an integral is as follows.

(i) Identify the independent variable of interest.

(ii) Set up a discrete model by dividing the area into narrow strips, whose long boundaries correspond to constant values for this independent variable.

(iii)Find an estimate for the required quantity in each strip.

(iv)Add up the required quantities for each strip to obtain a summation.

(v) Increase the number of strips indefinitely (and correspondingly let the width of each strip tend to zero) to obtain a continuous model based on a definite integral.

◇   The narrow strips into which the region is divided may be straight or annular, depending on the shape of the region involved.

Exercises for Section 5

Exercise 5.1

A biologist is studying the ecology of an insect species in a small region of meadow adjacent to a stream. The region can be modelled as a rectangle $OABC$, as shown in Figure 5.7, with width $OA = 12\,\text{m}$ and length $OC = 20\,\text{m}$. The stream runs along side OC of the region.

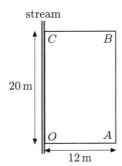

Figure 5.7

The biologist has established that the species population density depends only on distance from the stream, and that the number $s(x)$ of the species per square metre can be modelled by

$$s(x) = 12x - x^2 \quad (0 \le x \le 12),$$

where x measures distance away from the stream.

The biologist now wishes to estimate the total number of the species in this region of meadow. By setting up a definite integral, find the value of this total number as predicted by the model.

Exercise 5.2

Suppose that the region of land occupied by a town is modelled by a circle of radius R km. The population density decreases with distance from the centre, and is modelled by assuming that this decrease is linear, with density p_0 at the centre and density 0 at the periphery.

(a) Taking r km to denote distance from the centre, find an expression for the population density $p(r)$ people per km^2 within the town.

(b) Find an expression, involving a definite integral, for the population living within L km of the centre (where $L \le R$).

(c) Find an expression for the population living more than one kilometre from the centre (assuming that $R > 1$).

(d) According to this model, how many people live more than one kilometre from the centre of the town when $p_0 = 10\,000$ and $R = 3$?

Summary of Chapter C2

In Activities 1.3 and 3.4 you were asked to summarise some mathematics which had just been introduced. Now is a good time to look back at these summaries and see how well they reflect what you have learned in the chapter as a whole and how you achieved that learning.

Activity 6.1 Ways of working on mathematics

Look back at what you wrote in response to Activities 1.3 and 3.4.

Could you now make a clearer or fuller summary of either topic?

Can you identify any activities which helped your developing understanding, or any strategies you used to work on aspects of the chapter which you found difficult? For example, did listening to the audio tape or using Mathcad help clarify something which had not been obvious in the text. What were the roles of making summaries, doing exercises or reading notation aloud?

If there are particular ways of clarifying the material, of getting yourself 'unstuck,' that you want to use more often, make a note to yourself on Learning File Sheet 3.

The major concepts covered by this chapter are:

◇ what integration is, both as the 'undoing' of differentiation (Section 1) and as the limit of a sequence of sums (Section 4);

◇ how to integrate functions, either 'by hand' (Section 1) or using Mathcad (Section 2);

◇ how to solve simple differential equations, and where they may arise in mathematical modelling (Section 3);

◇ how to find definite integrals, either 'by hand' or using Mathcad (Section 4);

◇ how to find the area under the graph of a function, using a definite integral (Section 4);

◇ how definite integrals may be set up and put to use in mathematical models (Section 5).

Learning outcomes

You have been working towards the following learning outcomes.

Terms to know and use

Integration, an integral, the indefinite integral, arbitrary constant, constant of integration, integral sign, integrand, differential equation, first-order, second-order, general solution, particular solution, initial condition, initial-value problem, exponential growth/decay, exponential model, proportionate growth rate, doubling time, decay rate, half-life, area under a graph, definite integral, limits of integration, upper/lower limit, dummy variable, area-so-far function.

Symbols and notation to know and use

◇ $\int f(x)\,dx$ or $\int f$ (indefinite integral);

◇ $[F(x)]_a^b$ or $[F]_a^b$ (function evaluated from a to b);

◇ $\int_a^b f(x)\,dx$ or $\int_a^b f$ (definite integral).

Ideas to be aware of

◇ That *the indefinite* integral is a family of functions, *an* integral is a single function and a *definite* integral is a number.

◇ That integration is both an 'undoing' of differentiation and a limit of a sequence of sums, with these two interpretations being linked by the Fundamental Theorem of Calculus.

◇ That definite integrals represent areas under graphs where the integrand is non-negative.

◇ What differential equations and integration can be used for.

◇ That for motion with constant acceleration, the position and velocity can be related directly to each other.

◇ What mathematical modelling is, and how the modelling cycle is used.

Mathematical skills

◇ Integrate 'by hand' any function of a type shown in Table 1.1 on page 20. Also, integrate any constant multiple, a sum or difference, or a sum of constant multiples of those same functions. This applies to finding both indefinite and definite integrals.

◇ Integrate or solve differential equations using the 'guess and check' approach, where appropriate.

◇ Evaluate definite integrals.

◇ Use integration to find an area under the graph of a function.

Mathcad skills

◇ Type expressions to be integrated (or otherwise manipulated) directly into Mathcad, without the use of a prepared file.

◇ Apply Mathcad to integrate an expression with respect to a specified variable, by using the $\int$ icon on the palette and Evaluate Symbolically or Simplify from the Symbolic menu.

◇ Remember that what Mathcad outputs as an 'indefinite integral' is an integral without an arbitrary constant.

◇ Apply Mathcad to find a definite integral symbolically, by using the $\int_a^b$ icon on the palette and Evaluate Symbolically or Simplify from the Symbolic menu.

◇ Apply Mathcad to find a definite integral numerically, by using the $\int_a^b$ icon on the palette and then the '=' icon.

Modelling skills

◇ Appreciate that both differential equations and definite integrals can arise in the process of setting up mathematical models.

◇ Use the model of constant acceleration, where appropriate, for an object in one-dimensional motion.

◇ Use the model of exponential growth or decay in appropriate circumstances.

◇ Set up an integral as a continuous model which is the limit of discrete approximations.

Learning skills

◇ Be prepared to have your understanding of a concept reinforced by seeing it from a different viewpoint.

◇ Reflect on what you are learning in order to make sense of it.

◇ Identify points which are not clear to you as you study material and find strategies for obtaining clarification.

Investigating processes to aid understanding

◇ Be prepared to write down 'candidate' answers for integrals, which can then be checked for correctness by differentiating them.

◇ Develop a visual sense of what is involved in obtaining a definite integral by taking the limit of a sequence of sums.

Solutions to Activities

Solution 1.1

In each case, the result of differentiating the given velocity function is

$$\frac{dv}{dt} = 9.8.$$

Solution 1.4

In each solution, c is an arbitrary constant.

(a) $\int \left(x + 2x^2\right) dx = \frac{1}{2}x^2 + \frac{2}{3}x^3 + c$

(b) $\int \left(\frac{1}{x} + \exp(2x)\right) dx = \ln x + \frac{1}{2}\exp(2x) + c$

(c) $\int (a\sin(\omega t) + b\cos(\omega t))\, dt$

$\quad = \frac{b}{\omega}\sin(\omega t) - \frac{a}{\omega}\cos(\omega t) + c$

(d) $\int \left(x^{5/3} + x^{-1/2} + \exp(-2x)\right) dx$

$\quad = \frac{3}{8}x^{8/3} + 2x^{1/2} - \frac{1}{2}\exp(-2x) + c$

(e) $\int (x+1)^2\, dx = \int (x^2 + 2x + 1)\, dx$

$\quad = \frac{1}{3}x^3 + x^2 + x + c$

Solution 1.5

(a) $\int \cosh x\, dx = \int \frac{\exp(x) + \exp(-x)}{2}\, dx$

$\quad = \frac{\exp(x) - \exp(-x)}{2} + c$

$\quad = \sinh x + c,$

where c is an arbitrary constant.

(b) $\int \sinh x\, dx = \int \frac{\exp(x) - \exp(-x)}{2}\, dx$

$\quad = \frac{\exp(x) + \exp(-x)}{2} + c$

$\quad = \cosh x + c,$

where c is an arbitrary constant.

Solution 1.6

(a) From the formula

$$\cos(2x) = 2\cos^2 x - 1,$$

we have

$$\int \cos^2 x\, dx = \int \left(\tfrac{1}{2} + \tfrac{1}{2}\cos(2x)\right) dx$$

$$= \tfrac{1}{2}x + \tfrac{1}{4}\sin(2x) + c,$$

where c is an arbitrary constant.

(b) From the formula

$$\cos 2x = 1 - 2\sin^2 x,$$

we have

$$\int \sin^2 x\, dx = \int \left(\tfrac{1}{2} - \tfrac{1}{2}\cos(2x)\right) dx$$

$$= \tfrac{1}{2}x - \tfrac{1}{4}\sin(2x) + c,$$

where c is an arbitrary constant.

Solution 3.1

(a) The general solution of the equation

$$\frac{dP}{dt} = \cos t + 2$$

is

$$P = \int (\cos t + 2)\, dt$$

$$= \sin t + 2t + c,$$

where c is an arbitrary constant.

(b) The general solution of the equation

$$\frac{dy}{dx} = \exp(4x) + \exp(-4x)$$

is

$$y = \int (\exp(4x) + \exp(-4x))\, dx$$

$$= \tfrac{1}{4}\exp(4x) - \tfrac{1}{4}\exp(-4x) + c,$$

where c is an arbitrary constant.

(c) The general solution of the equation

$$\frac{dz}{du} = 3\sin(\omega u)$$

is

$$z = \int 3\sin(\omega u)\, du$$

$$= -\frac{3}{\omega}\cos(\omega u) + c,$$

where c is an arbitrary constant.

Solution 3.2

(a) The general solution of the equation

$$\frac{ds}{dt} = 9.8t + 3$$

is

$$s = \int (9.8t + 3) \, dt$$
$$= 9.8 \times \tfrac{1}{2} t^2 + 3t + c$$
$$= 4.9t^2 + 3t + c,$$

where c is an arbitrary constant.

(b) On applying the initial condition $s = 0$ when $t = 0$, we find that $c = 0$. Hence the position function of the bungee jumper while in free fall is

$$s = 4.9t^2 + 3t.$$

After 2 seconds, the jumper has fallen a distance

$$4.9 \times 2^2 + 3 \times 2 = 25.6 \, \text{m}.$$

Solution 3.3

In each case, we use the general solution of the differential equation obtained in Solution 3.1, where c is an arbitrary constant.

(a) The general solution is

$$P = \sin t + 2t + c.$$

From the initial condition

$$P = 4 \text{ when } t = 0,$$

we find that $c = 4$, and so the solution of the initial-value problem is

$$P = \sin t + 2t + 4.$$

(b) The general solution is

$$y = \tfrac{1}{4} \exp(4x) - \tfrac{1}{4} \exp(-4x) + c.$$

From the initial condition

$$y = -1 \text{ when } x = 0,$$

we find that $c = -1$, and so the solution of the initial-value problem is

$$y = \tfrac{1}{4} \exp(4x) - \tfrac{1}{4} \exp(-4x) - 1.$$

(c) The general solution is

$$z(u) = -\frac{3}{\omega} \cos(\omega u) + c.$$

From the initial condition

$$z(0) = \omega^{-1},$$

we find that

$$c = \frac{1}{\omega} - \left(-\frac{3}{\omega} \right) = \frac{4}{\omega},$$

and so the solution of the initial-value problem is

$$z(u) = \frac{4}{\omega} - \frac{3}{\omega} \cos(\omega u).$$

Solution 3.5

The two given equations are

$$v = at + v_0,$$
$$s = \tfrac{1}{2} at^2 + v_0 t + s_0.$$

On solving the first equation for t, we have

$$t = \frac{v - v_0}{a}.$$

Using this to substitute for t in the second equation gives

$$s = \tfrac{1}{2} a \left(\frac{v - v_0}{a} \right)^2 + v_0 \left(\frac{v - v_0}{a} \right) + s_0.$$

After multiplying through by $2a$, we obtain

$$2as = (v - v_0)^2 + 2v_0(v - v_0) + 2as_0$$
$$= v^2 - v_0^2 + 2as_0,$$

which may also be written as

$$2as - v^2 = 2as_0 - v_0^2.$$

Solution 3.6

(a) We assume that the aircraft moves in a straight line, and brakes with constant deceleration. Equation (3.8) is

$$2as - v^2 = 2as_0 - v_0^2.$$

Choosing the positive direction in the direction of motion of the aircraft, with the origin at its point of touch-down, we have $s_0 = 0$ and $v_0 = 70$, giving

$$2as - v^2 = -70^2.$$

For the minimum deceleration, we need $v = 5$ when $s = 550$. On putting these values into the equation above and solving for a, we obtain

$$a = \frac{5^2 - 70^2}{2 \times 550} = -\frac{195}{44} \simeq -4.43.$$

The minimum required magnitude of acceleration is therefore $4.43 \, \text{m s}^{-2}$.

(b) The corresponding time of travel along the runway is obtained from equation (3.3), which gives

$$t = \frac{v - v_0}{a}$$
$$= -\frac{44(5 - 70)}{195} = \frac{44}{3} \simeq 14.7 \text{ seconds.}$$

Solution 3.8

An increase of 3% per year corresponds to a proportionate growth rate of $k = 0.03$ year^{-1}, so with $P_0 = 10$ million $= 10^7$, the population after time t years is given by

$$P = 10^7 \exp(0.03t).$$

After 10 years, the predicted population is

$$P = 10^7 \exp(0.3) \simeq 1.34986 \times 10^7$$
$$= 13.5 \text{ million (to 3 s.f.).}$$

Solution 3.9

(a) The general solution of the differential equation

$$\frac{dy}{dx} = 2y$$

is

$$y = A \exp(2x),$$

where A is an arbitrary constant. Since $y = 100$ when $x = 0$, the particular solution is

$$y = 100 \exp(2x).$$

(b) The general solution of the differential equation

$$\frac{dv}{dt} = -3v$$

is

$$v = A \exp(-3t),$$

where A is an arbitrary constant. Since $v = 15$ when $t = 0$, the particular solution is

$$v = 15 \exp(-3t).$$

Solution 3.10

(a) The population P depends upon the time t (in days) according to the exponential model, so we have

$$P = P_0 \exp(kt),$$

where $P_0 = 50$. The value of the proportionate growth rate k is not stated directly, but it is given that $P = 1000$ when $t = 1$, from which we deduce that

$$1000 = 50 \exp k,$$

that is,

$$k = \ln\left(\frac{1000}{50}\right) = \ln 20$$
$$= 3.00 \text{ (to 3 s.f.).}$$

The population function is therefore

$$P = 50 \exp(t \ln 20).$$

(b) The population after two days is found by putting $t = 2$ into the last equation, to obtain

$$P = 50 \exp(2 \ln 20) = 50 \exp(\ln(20^2))$$
$$= 50 \times 20^2 = 20\,000.$$

(In fact, this part can be answered without first finding the value of k. The factor by which the population is multiplied is the same over each day. Hence the 20-fold increase over the first day is repeated for the second day.)

(c) The doubling time is

$$T = \frac{\ln 2}{k} = \frac{\ln 2}{\ln 20} \simeq 0.23 \text{ days,}$$

which is about $5\frac{1}{2}$ hours.

Solution 3.11

The radioactive decay of carbon 14 can be modelled by the differential equation

$$\frac{dm}{dt} = -\lambda m,$$

whose solution is

$$m = m_0 \exp(-\lambda t).$$

The half-life $T = 5570$ years leads to a value for the decay rate of

$$\lambda = \frac{\ln 2}{5570} \simeq 1.24 \times 10^{-4} \text{ year}^{-1}.$$

At the present time, we have $m/m_0 = 15\% = 0.15$, where $t = 0$ is the time at which the animal died. This gives the equation

$$0.15 = \exp\left(-\frac{t \ln 2}{5570}\right),$$

where t is the time which has elapsed since the death of the animal. The solution is

$$t = -\frac{5570 \ln 0.15}{\ln 2} \simeq 15\,200 \text{ years.}$$

Solution 4.1

(a) The area required is that of a rectangle, with base 5 and height 3, so its area is $3 \times 5 = 15$.

(b) Since $f(x) = 3$ is a constant function, an integral is

$$F(x) = 3x.$$

(Any choice of the form $F(x) = 3x + c$, where c is a constant, is correct here, but $F(x) = 3x$ is the simplest choice.) Then we have

$$F(5) - F(0) = 15 - 0 = 15,$$

which is the same value as for the area calculated in (a).

Solution 4.2

(a) The area required is that of a trapezium, which may be regarded as the sum of a rectangle, with base $2 - (-1) = 3$ and height $f(-1) = 1$, and a triangle with the same base and with height $f(2) - f(-1) = 7 - 1 = 6$. The area is therefore

$$3 \times 1 + \tfrac{1}{2} \times 3 \times 6 = 12.$$

(b) An integral of $f(x) = 2x + 3$ is

$$F(x) = x^2 + 3x.$$

(Any choice of the form $F(x) = x^2 + 3x + c$, where c is a constant, is also correct here.) Then we have

$$F(2) - F(-1)$$
$$= (2^2 + 3 \times 2) - ((-1)^2 + 3 \times (-1)) = 12,$$

which is the same value as for the area calculated in (a).

Solution 4.3

(a) $[\tfrac{1}{2}x^2]_3^5 = \tfrac{1}{2} \times 5^2 - \tfrac{1}{2} \times 3^2 = \tfrac{1}{2}(25 - 9) = 8.$

(b) $[\cos x]_0^{2\pi} = \cos(2\pi) - \cos 0 = 1 - 1 = 0.$

(c) $[\exp x]_{-1}^1 = \exp 1 - \exp(-1) = e - e^{-1} \simeq 2.35.$

Solution 4.4

(a) An integral of x^2 is $\tfrac{1}{3}x^3$, so we have

$$\int_{-1}^1 x^2 \, dx = [\tfrac{1}{3}x^3]_{-1}^1$$
$$= \tfrac{1}{3} \times 1^3 - \tfrac{1}{3} \times (-1)^3 = \tfrac{2}{3}.$$

(b) An integral of $\exp t$ is $\exp t$, so we have

$$\int_0^2 \exp t \, dt = [\exp t]_0^2$$
$$= e^2 - e^0 = e^2 - 1 \simeq 6.39.$$

(c) An integral of $1/u$ is $\ln u$ (for $u > 0$), so we have

$$\int_1^4 \frac{1}{u} \, du = [\ln u]_1^4$$
$$= \ln 4 - \ln 1 = \ln 4 \simeq 1.39.$$

Solution 4.5

(a) The area required is

$$\int_{-1}^1 x^2 \, dx,$$

whose value you found in Activity 4.4(a) to be $\tfrac{2}{3}$.

(b) The area required is

$$\int_0^{2/3} \exp(-3t) \, dt = [-\tfrac{1}{3} \exp(-3t)]_0^{2/3}$$
$$= -\tfrac{1}{3}e^{-2} - (-\tfrac{1}{3}e^0)$$
$$= \tfrac{1}{3}(1 - e^{-2}) \simeq 0.288.$$

(c) Using the integral given for $\ln u$, the area required is

$$\int_1^2 \ln u \, du = [u(\ln u - 1)]_1^2$$
$$= 2(\ln 2 - 1) - 1(\ln 1 - 1)$$
$$= 2 \ln 2 - 1 \simeq 0.386.$$

Solution 4.6

(a) The function $f(x) = x$ takes negative values for $x < 0$, so is negative on part of the interval $[-1, 1]$. Thus the integral

$$\int_{-1}^1 x \, dx$$

does not represent an area.

(b) The function $f(x) = x^2$ is zero at $x = 0$, but is otherwise positive. Hence the integral

$$\int_{-1}^1 x^2 \, dx$$

represents the area under the graph of x^2 from -1 to 1. (In fact, you found this area in Activity 4.5(a).)

(c) The function $f(x) = \cos x$ is negative for $\pi/2 < x \le 3\pi/4$. Thus the integral

$$\int_0^{3\pi/4} \cos x \, dx$$

does not represent an area.

Solution 5.2

The definite integral is

$$\int_0^3 \cos\left(\frac{\pi y}{6}\right) dy = \left[\frac{6}{\pi}\sin\left(\frac{\pi y}{6}\right)\right]_0^3$$
$$= \frac{6}{\pi}\left(\sin\left(\frac{\pi}{2}\right) - \sin 0\right) = \frac{6}{\pi}.$$

Hence we have

$$\frac{6p_0}{\pi} = 1750,$$

leading to

$$p_0 = \frac{1750\pi}{6} \simeq 916.$$

Solution 5.3

The argument is identical to that for the whole town, except that now we have $Nh = 1$ and correspondingly the upper limit of integration is altered to 1. The population within one kilometre of the road AB is therefore

$$20p_0 \int_0^1 \cos\left(\frac{\pi y}{6}\right) dy = 20p_0 \left[\frac{6}{\pi}\sin\left(\frac{\pi y}{6}\right)\right]_0^1$$
$$= \frac{120p_0}{\pi}\sin\left(\frac{\pi}{6}\right) = \frac{60p_0}{\pi}.$$

Taking $p_0 = 1750\pi/6$, as found in Activity 5.2, this becomes 17 500. So the model predicts that 17 500 people are living within one kilometre of the road.

Solution 5.4

The population density function is again symmetric about $y = 0$, since $p(y) = p(-y)$. It therefore suffices once more to consider just the half of the town for which $0 \le y \le 3$, and then to double the result.

The argument leading up to equation (5.3) on page 61 applies once more. On putting

$$p(y) = p_0 \exp(-y)$$

and doubling the definite integral, the total population of the town is given by

$$20p_0 \int_0^3 \exp(-y)\, dy = 20p_0 [-\exp(-y)]_0^3$$
$$= 20p_0(1 - e^{-3}).$$

Putting this equal to 20 000 and solving for p_0, we obtain

$$p_0 = \frac{20\,000}{20(1 - e^{-3})} = \frac{1000}{1 - e^{-3}} \simeq 1052.$$

The population within one kilometre of the road is then

$$20p_0 \int_0^1 \exp(-y)\, dy = 20p_0 [-\exp(-y)]_0^1$$
$$= 20p_0(1 - e^{-1})$$
$$= \frac{20\,000(1 - e^{-1})}{1 - e^{-3}} \simeq 13\,300.$$

The model estimates that, thirty years ago, there were about 13 300 people living within one kilometre of the road.

Solution 5.5

The area of the circle is

$$\int_0^R 2\pi r \, dr = [\pi r^2]_0^R = \pi R^2.$$

Solution 5.6

As just verified in the text and Solution 5.5, the area of the circular cross-section of a pipe of radius $R\,$m is $\pi R^2\,$m^2. Hence the volume flow rate through the pipe is $\pi v_0 R^2\,$m^{3}s^{-1}.

Solution 5.7

(a) On putting $r = 0$ in equation (5.4), we have $v(0) = v_0$, so that v_0 is the velocity of the water along the central axis of the pipe.

(b) At the pipe wall we have $r = R$, and $v(R) = 0$. The velocity at the pipe wall is zero. (This is due to the viscosity of the water, which causes it to 'stick' to the wall of the pipe.)

(c) The radial coordinate r takes only non-negative values, so the graph is the half-parabola shown below.

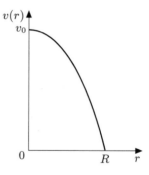

Figure S.1

(A picture of the variation of velocity across any circular cross-section of the pipe is obtained on rotating this curve through one revolution around the vertical axis.)

Solution 5.8

(a) There are N annular strips of width h, and the circular cross-section has radius R, so that $Nh = R$.

(b) The $(i+1)$th strip has internal circumference $2\pi ih$ and thickness h, so its approximate area is $(2\pi ih)h$.

(c) At $r = ih$ (the inside boundary of the $(i+1)$th strip) the velocity is $v(ih)$.

(d) From (b) and (c), the approximate volume flow rate across the $(i+1)$th strip is $2\pi ih\, v(ih)h$.

(e) The approximate volume flow rate across the whole cross-section of the pipe is obtained by summing the answer to (d) over all N strips, to give

$$\sum_{i=0}^{N-1} 2\pi ih\, v(ih)h, \quad \text{where } Nh = R.$$

This sum can also be written as

$$\sum_{i=0}^{N-1} 2\pi r_i v(r_i)\delta r,$$

where $r_i = ih$ and $\delta r = h$.

(f) On taking the limit of the answer in (e) as $N \to \infty$, we have that the volume flow rate is

$$2\pi \int_0^R rv(r)\,dr = \lim_{N\to\infty} \left[\sum_{i=0}^{N-1} 2\pi ih\, v(ih)h \right],$$

where $Nh = R$.

(g) On substituting the particular expression given for $v(r)$, the integral to be evaluated for the volume flow rate is

$$
2\pi v_0 \int_0^R r\left(1 - \left(\frac{r}{R}\right)^2\right) dr
$$
$$
= 2\pi v_0 \int_0^R \left(r - \frac{r^3}{R^2}\right) dr
$$
$$
= 2\pi v_0 \left[\frac{r^2}{2} - \frac{r^4}{4R^2}\right]_0^R
$$
$$
= 2\pi v_0 \left(\frac{R^2}{2} - \frac{R^2}{4}\right) = \tfrac{1}{2}\pi v_0 R^2.
$$

Solutions to Exercises

Solution 1.1

In each solution, c is an arbitrary constant.

(a) $\int t\sqrt{t}\,dt = \int t^{3/2}\,dt$

$\qquad = \frac{2}{5}t^{5/2} + c$

(b) $\int \left(\frac{3}{y^4} + 5\sin(5y)\right)dy = \int (3y^{-4} + 5\sin(5y))\,dy$

$\qquad\qquad = -y^{-3} - \cos(5y) + c$

(c) $\int 2\cos\left(\frac{s}{7}\right)ds = 14\sin\left(\frac{s}{7}\right) + c.$

(d) $\int \left(\frac{3}{v} + \exp(3v)\right)dv = 3\ln v + \frac{1}{3}\exp(3v) + c$

(e) $\int \exp(1+2x)\,dx = \int e^{1+2x}\,dx$

$\qquad\qquad = \int e^1 e^{2x}\,dx$

$\qquad\qquad = \frac{1}{2}e^1 e^{2x} + c$

$\qquad\qquad = \frac{1}{2}\exp(1+2x) + c$

Solution 3.1

(a) The general solution of the equation

$$\frac{dy}{dx} = x^3 - 1$$

is

$$y = \int (x^3 - 1)\,dx$$

$$= \frac{1}{4}x^4 - x + c,$$

where c is an arbitrary constant. From the initial condition $y = 5$ when $x = 0$, we find that $c = 5$, and so the solution of the initial-value problem is

$$y = \frac{1}{4}x^4 - x + 5.$$

(b) The general solution of the equation

$$v'(t) = 4\cos(2t) - 5\sin(3t)$$

is

$$v(t) = \int (4\cos(2t) - 5\sin(3t))\,dt$$

$$= 2\sin(2t) + \frac{5}{3}\cos(3t) + c,$$

where c is an arbitrary constant. From the initial condition $v(0) = 1$, we find that

$$c = 1 - \frac{5}{3} = -\frac{2}{3},$$

and so the solution of the initial-value problem is

$$v(t) = 2\sin(2t) + \frac{5}{3}\cos(3t) - \frac{2}{3}.$$

Solution 3.2

(a) Choose the direction of motion to be positive in the direction vertically upwards, with origin at the point of projection of the ball. Then, ignoring air resistance, the ball will have constant acceleration $-g$.

The ball attains its maximum height when its velocity is zero. The most direct approach to finding this height is to apply equation (3.8). We have

$$2as - v^2 = 2as_0 - v_0^2,$$

where $a = -g = -9.8$, $s_0 = 0$ and $v_0 = 25$. Thus when $v = 0$, we obtain

$$s = -\frac{v_0^2}{2a} = \frac{25^2}{2 \times 9.8} \simeq 31.9,$$

so the maximum height reached by the ball is $31.9\,\text{m}$ above its point of projection.

(b) The ball returns to its point of projection when it reaches $s = 0$ for the second time. According to equation (3.4), we have

$$s = \tfrac{1}{2}at^2 + v_0 t + s_0,$$

but with $a = -9.8$, $v_0 = 25$ and $s_0 = 0$, this becomes

$$s = 25t - 4.9t^2 = t(25 - 4.9t).$$

Thus $s = 0$ either at $t = 0$ (which is when the ball is first projected) or at

$$t = \frac{25}{4.9} \simeq 5.1,$$

so the ball returns to the point of projection after 5.1 seconds.

(c) The ball is $20\,\text{m}$ above its point of projection when $s = 20$, that is, when

$$20 = 25t - 4.9t^2.$$

The quadratic equation for t is

$$4.9t^2 - 25t + 20 = 0,$$

which has solution

$$t = \frac{25 \pm \sqrt{25^2 - 4 \times 4.9 \times 20}}{2 \times 4.9} = \frac{25 \pm \sqrt{233}}{9.8},$$

that is, $t \simeq 1.0$ and $t \simeq 4.1$. Therefore the ball is $20\,\text{m}$ above its point of projection at about $1.0\,\text{s}$ and $4.1\,\text{s}$ after it has been projected.

Solution 3.3

The mass m of carbon present in the wood at time t is described by the equation

$$m = m_0 \exp(-\lambda t),$$

where m_0 is the initial amount (at the time $t = 0$ when the wood became buried). The decay rate for carbon 14, with half-life 5570 years, was found in the solution to Activity 3.11 to be

$$\lambda = \frac{\ln 2}{5570} \simeq 1.24 \times 10^{-4} \text{ year}^{-1}.$$

From the analysis of the sample, we have $m/m_0 = 0.6$, which gives the equation

$$0.6 = \exp\left(-\frac{t \ln 2}{5570}\right),$$

for the age t of the piece of wood. The solution is

$$t = -\frac{5570 \ln 0.6}{\ln 2} \simeq 4\,100 \text{ years.}$$

Solution 4.1

(a) An integral of $\cos(5x) + 2\sin(5x)$ is $\frac{1}{5}\sin(5x) - \frac{2}{5}\cos(5x)$, so we have

$$\int_0^{\pi/4} (\cos(5x) + 2\sin(5x))\,dx$$

$$= \left[\frac{1}{5}\sin(5x) - \frac{2}{5}\cos(5x)\right]_0^{\pi/4}$$

$$= \left(\frac{1}{5}\sin(\tfrac{5}{4}\pi) - \frac{2}{5}\cos(\tfrac{5}{4}\pi)\right) - \left(\frac{1}{5}\sin 0 - \frac{2}{5}\cos 0\right)$$

$$= \frac{1}{5}\left(-1/\sqrt{2} - 2\left(-1/\sqrt{2}\right) - (-2)\right)$$

$$= \frac{1}{5}\left(1/\sqrt{2} + 2\right) \simeq 0.541.$$

(b) An integral of $6u^{-2}$ is $-6u^{-1}$, so we have

$$\int_1^2 \frac{6}{u^2}\,du = \left[-\frac{6}{u}\right]_1^2$$

$$= -\frac{6}{2} - \left(-\frac{6}{1}\right) = 3.$$

(c) Using the integral given, we have

$$\int_0^\pi e^t \sin t\,dt$$

$$= \left[\frac{1}{2}e^t(\sin t - \cos t)\right]_0^\pi$$

$$= \frac{1}{2}e^\pi(\sin \pi - \cos \pi) - \frac{1}{2}e^0(\sin 0 - \cos 0)$$

$$= \frac{1}{2}(-(-1)e^\pi - (-1))$$

$$= \frac{1}{2}(e^\pi + 1) \simeq 12.1.$$

Solution 4.2

(a) The area required is

$$\int_1^2 2x^3\,dx = \left[\frac{1}{2}x^4\right]_1^2$$

$$= \frac{1}{2} \times 2^4 - \frac{1}{2} \times 1^4$$

$$= \frac{1}{2}(2^4 - 1) = \frac{15}{2}.$$

(b) The graph of the function given is a parabola which cuts the x-axis at $x = 0$ and $x = 3$, and is above the x-axis for $0 < x < 3$. The area required is therefore

$$\int_0^3 x(3 - x)\,dx = \int_0^3 (3x - x^2)\,dx$$

$$= \left[\frac{3}{2}x^2 - \frac{1}{3}x^3\right]_0^3$$

$$= \frac{3}{2} \times 3^2 - \frac{1}{3} \times 3^3$$

$$= \frac{27}{2} - 9 = \frac{9}{2}.$$

(c) Using the integral given, the area required is

$$\int_{-2}^2 \frac{1}{1 + x^2}\,dx = [\arctan x]_{-2}^2$$

$$= \arctan 2 - \arctan(-2)$$

$$= 2\arctan 2 \simeq 2.21.$$

Solution 5.1

The procedure for setting up integrals is given on page 62. The independent variable of interest here is x. Suppose that the region of meadow is divided into N strips, each of width h m and parallel to OC (see Figure S.2). Then we have $Nh = 12$.

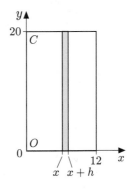

Figure S.2

Each strip has area $20h$ m^2. The $(i+1)$th strip extends from

$$x = ih \text{ to } x = (i+1)h \quad (i = 0, 1, 2, \ldots, N-1),$$

so that on the $(i+1)$th strip there are approximately

$$s(ih) \times 20h \text{ insects.}$$

For all of the N strips, this gives an estimate of

$$\sum_{i=0}^{N-1} 20s(ih)h, \quad \text{where } Nh = 12,$$

for the total number of insects. This sum can also be written as

$$\sum_{i=0}^{N-1} 20s(x_i)\delta x,$$

where $x_i = ih$ and $\delta x = h$. For the 'best estimate', take the limit of the sum as $N \to \infty$, to obtain

$$20 \int_0^{12} s(x)\, dx = \lim_{N\to\infty} \left[\sum_{i=0}^{N-1} 20s(ih)h \right],$$

where $Nh = 12$.

Putting $s(x) = 12x - x^2$, the total number of insects is estimated to be

$$20 \int_0^{12} (12x - x^2)\, dx = 20\left[6x^2 - \tfrac{1}{3}x^3\right]_0^{12}$$

$$= 20(6 \times 12^2 - \tfrac{1}{3} \times 12^3)$$

$$= 40 \times 12^2 = 5760.$$

The model predicts that the total population of the insect species within this region of meadow is 5800 (to 2 s.f.).

Solution 5.2

(a) Since $p(r)$ is a linear function, we have

$$p(r) = mr + c,$$

where m and c are constants. It is given that $p(0) = p_0$ and $p(R) = 0$, from which we have

$$p_0 = c \quad \text{and} \quad 0 = mR + c.$$

Thus $c = p_0$, $m = -p_0/R$ and

$$p(r) = p_0\left(1 - \frac{r}{R}\right) \quad (0 \le r \le R).$$

(b) Divide the circular area up to L km from the centre of the town into N annular strips of width h, so that $Nh = L$. The $(i+1)$th strip extends from $r = ih$ to $r = (i+1)h$, has internal circumference $2\pi ih$ and approximate area $(2\pi ih)h$. Hence the population living within the strip is approximately $2\pi ih\, p(ih)h$. On summing over all N strips, and then taking the limit of this sum as $N \to \infty$, the total population within L km of the centre is

$$2\pi \int_0^L rp(r)\, dr = \lim_{N\to\infty}\left[\sum_{i=0}^{N-1} 2\pi ih\, p(ih)h\right],$$

where $Nh = L$.

With $p(r)$ as found in (a), this is

$$2\pi p_0 \int_0^L r\left(1 - \frac{r}{R}\right) dr$$

$$= 2\pi p_0 \int_0^L \left(r - \frac{r^2}{R}\right) dr$$

$$= 2\pi p_0 \left[\frac{r^2}{2} - \frac{r^3}{3R}\right]_0^L$$

$$= 2\pi p_0 \left(\frac{L^2}{2} - \frac{L^3}{3R}\right).$$

(c) If $P(L)$ is the expression found in (b), then the population who live more than one kilometre from the centre is

$$P(R) - P(1)$$

$$= 2\pi p_0 \left(\left(\frac{R^2}{2} - \frac{R^3}{3R}\right) - \left(\frac{1}{2} - \frac{1}{3R}\right)\right)$$

$$= 2\pi p_0 \left(\frac{R^2}{6} - \frac{1}{2} + \frac{1}{3R}\right).$$

(d) If $p_0 = 10\,000$ and $R = 3$, then the population who live more than one kilometre from the centre is

$$2\pi \times 10\,000 \left(\frac{3^2}{6} - \frac{1}{2} + \frac{1}{3 \times 3}\right)$$

$$= 20\,000\pi \left(\frac{9}{6} - \frac{1}{2} + \frac{1}{9}\right)$$

$$= \frac{200\,000\pi}{9} \simeq 69\,800.$$